Pennsylvania Pasta with Cremini (see page 41)

A Cook's Book of
MUSHROOMS

WITH 100 RECIPES FOR COMMON AND UNCOMMON VARIETIES

Jack Czarnecki

Photographs by
Louis B. Wallach

ARTISAN
New York

This book is dedicated to my father

Text copyright © Jack Czarnecki
Photographs copyright © Louis B. Wallach

Editor: Ann ffolliott
Production director: Hope Koturo

Published in 1995 by Artisan,
a division of Workman Publishing Company, Inc.
708 Broadway   New York, NY 10003

Library of Congress Cataloging-in-Publication Data
Czarnecki, Jack.
A cook's book of mushrooms / by Jack Czarnecki : photographs by Louis B. Wallach.
Includes bibliographical references and index.
ISBN 1-885183-07-0
1. Cookery (Mushrooms)   2. Mushrooms, Edible.   3. Joe's (Restaurant).   I. Title.
TX804.C89   1995
641.6'58—dc20   *94-48906*

Printed in Japan
10   9   8   7   6   5   4   3   2   1
First Printing

CONTENTS

INTRODUCTION

BY THEIR INFINITE VARIETY and ability to delight the senses, mushrooms hold a mystical place in the culinary galaxy. From their first appearance as edibles at Egyptian, Greek, and Roman feasts, these humble fungi growing so close to or under the earth have carried an aura of another world, just beyond our understanding. In fact, until recently the generally mycophobic West has largely ignored fungi as food. It was not until the seventeenth century that the cultivation of mushrooms was attempted at all, after which their popularity became so widespread that mushroom cultivation was a source of even greater mystery, owing to the secretive nature of those who controlled the mushroom production. By contrast, shiitake have been cultivated in Japan for more than two thousand years, and in Asia mushrooms and some of their more esoteric cousins are viewed as beneficial to health as well as tasty. Many Japanese and Chinese people regard the healing powers of mushrooms as unquestioned. At this moment, several species of wood fungi are being tested in the United States for properties that are suspected of being effective against the greatest scourge of our age, the HIV virus. Several other species are seen as effective antitumor agents and anticoagulants, as well as favorable for bolstering the immune system in general. Shiitake have been shown to lower blood cholesterol in controlled tests, and the research continues on many other mushroom species, both here and in Japan and China. It is safe to say that in Asia, mushrooms are revered and consumed as the ultimate health food.

But to say that you should eat mushrooms only for nutritional reasons would be to overlook their real magic—the ability to transform and transcend ordinary food. Mushrooms sparkle in dishes heavy with meat or yawning from mundane vegetables. They transform a vegetarian diet so that you will forget you are not eating meat. Their flavor surprises and their texture intrigues, again and again.

This book is a highly personal account of some of my own experiences with mushrooms. Because mushrooms know no ethnic boundaries, I combine ingredients from different countries. Indeed, I view the world as a giant marketplace from which to pluck the ingredients for these cross-cultural dishes. At Joe's Restaurant, we call this cooking "freestyle," in that it reflects our freedom to enhance the flavors of mushrooms to the greatest extent possible. I encourage you to experiment in the same fashion.

In writing this book, I also give you some small sense of what it is like to be a mushroom hunter, especially in eastern Pennsylvania. The rain gods do not always smile on us, but after what can be years of mushroom deprivation, the excitement of the hunt and the satisfaction of the find are all the more acute. Dry summers spell gloom for the avid hunter. Even a brief shower can send hopes soaring, as baskets are hurriedly thrown into the back of the car. Here we truly hunt and it is not easy, but we do have fun. I want you to come along for a brief trek into our world, and visit my kitchen as we conjure up some mushroom magic.

About Common Names

This book is arranged according to several broad classifications of mushrooms, both wild and domestic. The chapters are based on those mushrooms that are best known for their pure culinary magic. Mushrooms have been collected for hundreds of years, and so their names have been adapted or shortened for common use. However, it is useful to remember from time to time that the lexicon of common names derives or departs from the scientific or taxonomic names, which are in Latin. For example, a chanterelle is *Cantharellus cibarius;* however certain other mushrooms, such as *Cantharellus lateritius,* may also be called a chanterelle. So by giving mushrooms common names we have developed a convenient but inexact and nonspecific practice of identification. In contrast, Latin names *are* specific; the species name refers to one mushroom and one mushroom alone. And, of course, not all mushrooms have common names. The more commonly a mushroom is gathered, the more likely it will have a generally accepted common name. Conversely, seldom-picked mushrooms are mostly referred to by their Latin names. There has been a tendency in the last few years to "force" common names onto the lesser picked species, but this seems foolish.

This book lists most mushrooms by their Latin names. I have used a common name only when I know the mushroom has really been called by that name by U.S. mushroom hunters, especially when the name will aid cooks in identifying the species in the field or market. Sometimes that means including French and Japanese names when those are used by suppliers. For example, *Grifola frondosa* is called hen-of-the-woods in English, but that name is seldom used by suppliers, who are more likely to refer to it by its Japanese name, maitake. I am sure I have missed some common designations, but I have tried to include as complete a list of common names as is currently available.

Keeping and Storing Mushrooms

Whether your mushrooms are domestic or wild, the first thing you should do when you get them into your kitchen is keep them cold until you are ready to use them. The issue of using plastic or paper bags (it doesn't matter) is irrelevant if the mushrooms rot before you start cooking. Cold air retards the natural enzymatic process that causes mushrooms to rot. The other factor that accelerates spoilage is moisture. If you are not going to use your mushrooms right away, keep them cold but *do not rinse them before storage.* Wash them just before using them. If you have basketfuls of wild mushrooms, you should follow one of the procedures for long-term storage: canning, salting, or drying. But the average haul of mushrooms from the woods or supermarket will keep for four or five days in the refrigerator. You may also freeze them for several days. If kept frozen for no more than two weeks, many mushrooms will defrost and be remarkably similar to fresh mushrooms. After two weeks, the mushrooms become limp and lifeless. By the way, those mushroom brushes are great for nails. A damp cloth works better to remove the dirt imbedded in mushrooms.

Dried mushrooms will keep for a long time in the kitchen cabinet, but there is a possibility that larvae will hatch and eat them. This can be prevented by keeping dried mushrooms in the freezer.

Cooking with Fresh Mushrooms

Most mushrooms have to be cleaned before using. If you are going to braise, stir-fry, or boil the mushrooms, or add them to a soup or stew, use the following method, which is also the first step if you are going to can or salt the mushrooms. First, cut off the bottom of the stem, because there is usually a concentration of dirt where the mushroom was below ground. Then, feel the mushroom and get an idea of how delicate it is. *Russulas* and hedgehogs, for example, are quite brittle so they must be handled carefully. The best way to clean mushrooms that break apart easily is to soak them in a tub of hot water. This loosens the dirt, needles, or leaves while at the same time makes the mushrooms more pliable and less likely to break apart. (The only mushrooms that you do not want to soak are medium to aged boletes, because the pores on the underside of the cap will absorb water and become mushy when cooked.) Even if the mushrooms are firm and pliable when fresh, soaking them in some warm or hot water is still a good idea for loosening the dirt. Let them sit in the water for about ten minutes (longer if the mushrooms are very cold and very dirty or coated with pine needles), then lift out the mushrooms one by one and scrape away the dirt with a paring knife while rinsing under warm water. You will be surprised at how much dirt is washed away just from rinsing under the tap.

If you plan to broil, grill, or dry your mushrooms you must proceed differently. Clean the dirt from the mushrooms as best as you can with a knife, then wipe the surface with a damp cloth to remove any stubborn dirt. *Never* wash or soak mushrooms if you are going to dry them. They may rot before they dry. You can use some water if you are going to grill or broil them, but do not let the mushroom absorb large amounts of water or they will get mushy while grilling.

Mushrooms are hard to burn when cooking since they are mostly liquid. But don't forget that the liquid contains a high concentration of mushroom flavor—what you might think of as a self-contained sauce or broth. Therefore, if you add fresh mushrooms to a stew or casserole—a simple method of adding character to a dish—adjust for additional thickening because the mushroom's liquid will thin the sauce. Braising mushrooms is one of my favorite cooking methods. Melt some butter in a large saucepan and sauté some onions in it. Add the mushrooms with just a tiny amount of water, cover, and let the mushrooms yield their liquid into the pan. Remove the lid after the mushrooms are submerged and season and thicken with a mixture of cornstarch and cold water to serve. You will need to add a little more water for drier mushrooms, such as polypores. This is simply one of the very best ways to enjoy fresh mushrooms, period.

If you want to stir-fry mushrooms you must remember two things. First, the mushrooms will give off a lot of liquid, so the heat must be fairly high. Second, you must thoroughly cook the mushrooms. The tendency in a stir-fried dish is to keep the ingredients crunchy and barely cooked, but this is not a good idea for wild mushrooms, which should *always be thoroughly cooked.* Wild mushrooms contain varying amounts of protein that the body cannot digest until it has been cooked.

Mushrooms have very subtle flavors. Sautéing them in onions and butter remains one of the best ways of preparing them. Some varieties, like shiitake, are enhanced by the addition of spices and herbs, but most mushrooms are not. Vinegar, wine, and lemon juice, while enhancing a dish as a whole, tend to diminish the flavor of mushrooms in inverse proportion to their concentration, so that pickled mushrooms rarely taste like mushrooms at all—even though they may taste great because of the flavor of the marinade. That is not to say that you should avoid acids such as wine; just be aware of their effect on the flavor of the mushrooms. And there are some exceptions to this. Chanterelles and certain types of oyster mushrooms contain some acidity themselves.

In matters of seasoning, be subtle. Garlic and mushrooms are great, but garlicky mushrooms all taste the same. Instead, savory is the best herb to use with mushrooms because it enhances their natural flavors. For seasoning mushrooms, I use what I call the "fungal holy trinity," a combination of salt, soy sauce, and sugar in modest amounts. If salt is used exclusively, the mushrooms take on a metallic flavor. Soy sauce enhances the flavor of mushrooms, but if soy sauce is used exclusively the mushrooms taste too much of soy. Finally, a tiny amount of sugar rounds out the sharpness from the salt and soy sauce. The dish should not taste sweet at all. The individual recipes in this book specify the proper amount of seasoning.

Cooking with Dried Mushrooms

Fresh mushrooms are characterized by a sweet nutty-buttery flavor with a wide spectrum of textures. Dried mushrooms are often thought of as embalmed versions of the fresh, with only water needed to bring them back to their original state. I'm sorry to report that with the exception of a few mushrooms, such as the *mousseron* or fairy ring mushroom *(Marasmius oreades),* no dried mushrooms can be reconstituted to anything resembling their fresh condition. Rather than bemoan that fact, you must think of dried mushrooms as herbs and spices rather than as fresh mushrooms, for the process of drying concentrates the flavor and reveals the robust intensity only hinted at in the fresh state. Of course, this is not true of all dried mushrooms. Sometimes the sweetness of a fresh mushroom is all it has to offer to the palate, and the dried version of the same mushroom yields little more than a bland broth. The best mushrooms for drying or for buying dried are morels, cèpes *(Bolitus edulis,* also known as porcini), and black chanterelles. Dried shiitakes are also good, and cloud ears are usually only available dried. Beyond these, the list drops off very fast. Dried oyster mushrooms, for example, are pleasant enough but downright ugly upon reconstitution, as are dried regular chanterelles. The primary criterion for good drying is the liquid that is left after reconstitution. If it is dark and fragrant, then the mushroom was worth drying. If it is pale and bland, then you might as well not have bothered. Still, it is always worth experimenting and I encourage you to do so.

Reconstituting dried mushrooms is simple. Place them in a saucepan, cover with water, and bring to a raging boil. Then reduce the heat and simmer for about twenty minutes. Soaking the mushrooms in warm water overnight, then throwing away the water, is cruel and unusual punishment for these intense little flavor enhancers. The magic is in the liquid, which should be used for intense consommé-style soups or as the base for a sauce. The reconstituted mushrooms can be chopped up for duxelles or sliced thin for a casserole, but not used as the primary focus of a dish. Flavor the mushroom liquid by following the recipes in this book that call for dried mushrooms.

Canned Mushrooms

Canned mushrooms have been processed at a high heat and therefore have lost much of their flavor. Canned straw mushrooms, cèpes, and chanterelles are fine added to stews. You do not need to make any adjustments for thickening, since these mushrooms have had most of their liquid cooked out of them during the canning process. Perhaps more than any other fungi, truffles suffer from canning because their flavor is the most volatile and likely to dissipate. Straw mushrooms are great for pickling and perfect in martinis. Canned cèpes are not easy to find, but they do retain a good texture and some flavor for sauces and stews. The same is true for chanterelles, which generally maintain their firm texture, although not their flavor.

Salted or Brined Mushrooms

Occasionally you will find mushrooms that have been salted or brined. Commercially these can come in plastic buckets or other containers without metal linings. The mushrooms must be well rinsed with running water in a colander so that the salt will be washed away. Chanterelles are the mushrooms most often sold like this. Once desalted, the mushrooms can be used in the same manner as canned mushrooms—although their texture will generally be superior. The process of brining is less damaging to the mushrooms because less heat is required.

Frozen Mushrooms

Frozen mushrooms are not generally available to consumers, but who knows when they will enter that market. The quality of frozen mushrooms has increased markedly in the past ten years. For example, most frozen wild varieties (mostly cèpes, but with a scattering of other wild types) are individually quick frozen, as opposed to mushrooms frozen and sold in a solid block. The quick-frozen mushrooms hold their shape better and are also processed almost on the spot. However, the longer mushrooms stay frozen, the more they deteriorate from either crystallization or freezer burn, so use them quickly. Also, it is better to thaw frozen mushrooms slowly in the refrigerator than let them sit out. Use frozen mushrooms as you would fresh, although there is some moisture loss in the frozen version.

Portobello

BUTTONS AND SAUCERS

The Genus Agaricus

E MBARRASSING — YES, THAT'S IT — embarrassing is the only way I can describe the feeling of harvesting a large bunch of *Agaricus* in the wild. I feel acutely self-conscious about this sudden mother lode of wild mushrooms, especially if it's a variety of giant prince or horse mushrooms. You see, mushroom hunters search for most of their treasures in dark forests under pine needles and fallen leaves, sometimes to return with nothing more to show for a day of hunting than some pine needles down the back of their shirts. Most trips yield few or no mushrooms, and even when he's successful, a mushroom hunter's basket may yield only small, bug-infested, or heavily soiled mushrooms that, in the end, have to be discarded. If you love aggravation and disappointment, then mushroom hunting is for you. But back to my story.

After days, months, and years of frustration there comes that one season when the rains fall at just the right time. As I drive along a road, I spot what look like softballs scattered in a field. Horses! Princes! Gold! I get out of the car at a half jog (mushroom hunters have no shame) and settle on my knees to fill my basket in two minutes. Of course, when I find *Agaricus* like this, I never have enough basket space. I end up piling them in the back of my station wagon.

Unless you are a wild-mushroom hunter who lives far from civilization, the chances are your first and most immediate image of mushrooms was formed by the button mushroom—the one found in supermarket produce sections. It is far and away the most heavily produced for domestic consumption. The history of its cultivation goes back to Paris in the late seventeenth century, when horticulturists discovered these mushrooms popping up in composted manure in which melons and pineapples were grown. By the early eighteenth century growers had established conditions for optimum growth, especially in damp and cool caves, and the domestication and commercialization of mushrooms were born. This industry was centered around Paris for many years and so the button mushroom was called the *champignon de Paris.*

The button mushroom is in the genus *Agaricus,* which contains some of the finest and most widely picked mushrooms in the world. Until the importation and subsequent cultivation in this country of the portobello, the average consumer in the United States was not able to enjoy the meaty succulence of the larger species of *Agaricus.* This is why I believe the portobello is the most exciting of the recently developed domestic mushrooms in this country.

The Character of Agaricus

The button mushroom is one of many species in the genus *Agaricus.* Characterized by light pinkish gills in their early development, the *Agaricus* mature to the point where the gills become a

It is late August. The chanterelles have not been plentiful this summer and besides a few old-man-of-the-woods, the forest has shown nothing but parched-looking polypores that reflect the thirsty ground below. In eastern Pennsylvania, each year brings its own combination of snow, wind, cold, heat, and rain. But it never brings the same combination of these.

I like to think of mushroom years the way vintners think of vintage years. They can tell you on what day the vines budded and how a late fall dry spell ripened their Chardonnay to a miraculous sugar level undreamed of in half a century. They will swirl their wine in a glass and consider the benign marriage of nature and intellect that produces such a luscious liquid offspring. Mushrooms have their good and bad vintages too, especially here in the East. Combinations of weather conditions produce or inhibit large outpourings of mycelial abundance in the forest, which make or break a year. A sodden spring followed by a dry summer can fail to coax even humble polypores from their sclerotic slumbers into the visible landscape of a summer forest.

You see, the one constant, the one condition that all mushrooms thirst for, is rain. And not just a random rain—no, it must be rain of a duration and quality that falls on the right days. Each variety has within its genetic network a timing device that tells it the moment of fruition has arrived. Some mushrooms, like morels, only fruit from the end of April until the middle of May. Other mushrooms, like the old-man-of-the-woods, can grow all summer. Others, like certain species of Russulas, only appear in the last week of August. But rain is the key. There are years when the sleeping spores remain dry and thus must remain in their nonfecund state deep in the soil, waiting for yet another year. If the rain does not come at the appointed and predestined period for that mushroom, its time will have passed for that year and fruiting will not occur.

The rain never falls the same way. Its intervals or duration or intensity are appointed by conditions hidden in the clouds and not known to us. So each year yields its unique outcropping of mushrooms depending on when the rain falls, and how much falls. Vintages of greatness are those years when our favorite varieties see the moisture they need soaking the ground during their time of potential fruition. And we all smile.

All of which is why we call rain "mushroom sunshine." It is to mushrooms what sunshine is to green plants. When the season begins in earnest, we are tuned several times a day to the local radio and television stations for weather reports. My father and I are on the phone to each other to discuss the possible areas in which we might look and the types of mushrooms we may find if the rain has been plentiful. Especially rewarding are those times when we get several days of hard rain together. Usually by the third day we are out in the woods looking for mushrooms—whether it is raining or not. There is a special feeling when you are in the woods looking for mushrooms while it is still pouring. I feel as if I am catching mushrooms in the process of being born. Here I am in the wet forest, being soaked by the same rain that is enriching the ground and causing the mushrooms to grow.

There is a unique appearance to mushrooms springing up in a wet forest. Caps soaked and gleaming, they create their own points of shimmering light in the dark woods. I am soaked to the skin, but making joyous discoveries one after another. My basket begins to fill with rich abundance of mushroom varieties freshly sprung out of the forest humus. Even if it is cold, I love that feeling of being there as they grow. The best mushroom hunts we have had were on cold, wet days. One by one, different mushroom hunters in our group and family would return—soaked, but with full baskets—to the car where my father was waiting. We would crowd in, close the doors, and while munching on ham sandwiches downed with warm Zinfandel, excitedly show off our baskets to one another in a contest of one-upmanship—all this to the sound of the rain pinging its tune on the roof of our car. And then there would be a moment of spontaneous silence while the rain continued and the odor of the day's riches began to permeate the air around us.

dark chocolate brown in most species. Generally, the smaller, closed caps are considered to be more desirable, while the open-capped mushrooms are thought to be too old. This is true, however, only if you are concerned with appearances. In fact, the older, more open caps are more intense in flavor, as evidenced by the portobello. Insofar as button mushrooms are concerned, those that are closed around the stem are prettier and during cooking they do not darken a broth or stew. The open-cap mushrooms are more flavorful, but because the gill color has changed from pink to brown, they will darken any dish in which they are cooked. So use closed caps in cream soups and opened caps in stews and ragouts or in recipes in which the darkening factor is not detrimental. Opened caps with dark gills are also good for duxelles. To complicate matters, many of the wild *Agaricus* species do not exhibit a closed-cap stage, even though the gills are still pink instead of dark brown.

The flavor of *Agaricus* is somewhat nutty and creamy when raw and becomes earthy and rich when cooked. This is characteristic of most mushrooms, because the cooking process releases the true flavors of mushrooms. Overall, *Agaricus,* especially the domestic variety, are much more flavorful than many other species. They will really add character to dishes to which they are added, unlike some wild varieties that are quite neutral in flavor.

Wild varieties of *Agaricus* tend to be softer and less "chalky" than button mushrooms and are also more pliable, but the flavor remains very similar. In all species, the stem is edible but generally firmer than the cap, which makes the stems suitable for grilling on their own, especially the larger varieties.

Agaricus are very good in stews, but the larger varieties are among the best mushrooms for grilling. They are also excellent sliced and sautéed, and the small, immature caps are ideal for pickling. The rich, earthy flavor of cooked *Agaricus* has led many cooks to add acids, such as lemon juice, to the dishes, but this should be done with restraint because acids tend to diminish the mushrooms' inherent flavors. As with other varieties of mushroom, *Agaricus* species tend to release quite a lot of liquid during cooking, which greatly enhances the flavor of finished soups and stews.

Varieties of Domestic Agaricus

Agaricus brunnescens (also *Agaricus bisporus*) Common name—button, supermarket mushroom, *champignon de Paris, champignon.* This is the common domestic mushroom. There are several important varieties that look slightly different, and cremini have a distinctly darker color. Varieties are: white (variety 'albidus'); cream (variety 'avellaneous'); cremini (variety 'bisporus'); giant cremini or portobello. The most popular of all the "wild" domestic mushrooms, portobellos are the only ones that possess the size and succulence of the larger wild mushrooms, such as porcini. Their recent popularity is due to their versatility, but they are also more tasty than their small cousins, supermarket button mushrooms, because the portobellos are sold when the caps are open and mature, the stage at which they are most flavorful. The portobello is the best domestic mushroom for grilling and roasting; it often grows to the size of a large saucer.

Agaricus bitorquis Common name—banded *Agaricus,* urban *Agaricus,* spring *Agaricus,* tork, Rodman's *Agaricus.* Some people think this is the best of the *Agaricus* species because of its meatiness; from a practical standpoint it is resistant to some viral infections that attack *Agaricus brunnescens.* It is much more commonly cultivated in Europe than in the United States, where it found wild (often in subterranean conditions and habitats). This mushroom, in fact, has been known to grow to full maturity and still be buried a foot underground! Max Lipp, an avid mushroom hunter, tells of finding hundreds of *A. bitorquis* one day in the Arizona desert, after spying a single old specimen that had just popped its head out of the red clay soil. All of the other mushrooms had to be dug out from underneath that clay with shovels. The only indication of their presence were cracks in the desert clay.

Agaricus subrufescens Common name—almond mushroom, slightly red mushroom. These are occasionally cultivated but apparently are less popular because of their rather intense almond aroma and flavor, although those who like the species are very enthusiastic about it. It is often found around greenhouses; the mushroom is quite rare in the wild except in southern California.

Varieties of Wild Agaricus

Agaricus campestris Common name—meadow mushroom, common field mushroom, pinkie, pink bottom, *psalliote des jardins, rose de pres, pratelle, potiron, Feldegerling, Wisenchampignon, haratake.* One of the most widely picked of all wild mushrooms, this mushroom species is softer and more pliable than the domestic *Agaricus brunnescens,* and the cap opens much more quickly to reveal its pink gills than the market variety does. The two mushrooms both taste of the distinctive *Agaricus* stamp, but the wild *A. campestris* is often more intense, especially if picked under optimum ripening conditions (plentiful moisture). The cap dries out fairly soon because of its exposed situation in fields and direct exposure to the midday sun, so these mushrooms should not be left to grow. They are wonderful in soups and stews.

Agaricus arvensis   Common name—horse mushroom, *psalliote des jacheres, boule de neige, paturon, Schaferling.* As you can probably guess from the name, this is a pretty sizable mushroom. Its cap can grow to anywhere from three to six inches in diameter. Horse mushrooms are excellent eating, with characteristics somewhat like *Agaricus bitorquis* but milder and far easier to find. I have worn out several sets of brake pads, frequently screeching to a halt from sixty miles an hour, whenever I catch a glimpse of these mushrooms on a lawn.

Agaricus augustus   Common name—prince. This is another one of the large wild field *Agaricus,* notable for its marshmallow-shaped cap when young. It is similar to *Agaricus arvensis.* It is very popular, with a rich and slightly almondlike taste and finish. It is delectable, and a great mushroom for grilling.

Agaricus osecanus   Common name—giant horse mushroom. Even larger than the horse mushrooms at times, this species is widely picked in California, where it appears abundantly in coastal pastures. I had the pleasure of finding a significant batch with Lee Yamada, of the Santa Cruz Mycological Society, one afternoon when we also found a huge batch of chanterelles. These are considered not as desirable for eating as the horse or prince, however.

Agaricus bernardii   Common name—salt-loving *Agaricus.* Generally smaller than the other wild *Agaricus* species, these mushrooms are not preferred by everyone because they have a metallic aftertaste. However, friends in California eat them often and consider them choice.

Agaricus lilaceps   Common name—giant cypress *Agaricus.* Another *Agaricus* common around Monterey Bay in California. They are considered choice, but too firm for some if not thoroughly cooked.

Agaricus silvicola   Common name—woodland *Agaricus,* silvan agaric. Another choice but smaller *Agaricus,* it grows very robustly in California, but is much more delicate in appearance when found in the East. They are easy and quick to cook, but they can appear very similar to deadly white *Amanitas,* which grow at the same time in the summer in eastern Pennsylvania.

Agaricus perobscurus   Common name—princess. These are similar to prince mushrooms but do not usually grow to their size. Similar in flavor but milder.

THE AGONY AND ECSTASY, AND ANGELS' STOMP

A friend called the other day to thank me for taking him mushroom hunting for the first time. It had been a good trip and we had found about one hundred mushrooms on that expedition. I paused for a moment and experienced a sudden attack of frankness, a weakness that says more about my impulsiveness than my intelligence. "Don't thank me," I replied. "What I've given you is hours, if you're smart, and years if you're not, of frustration and desperation that you'll experience trying to repeat a great mushroom-hunting trip. If you're doing it years from now and still feel the same way, call me up." I didn't mean to sound so discouraging because I really do love hunting mushrooms, but I wanted him to know that not every trip was going to be that successful.

My father likes to recall how he got interested in mushrooms. He used to go into the woods every fall with my grandmother to pick several varieties of mushrooms. One year the mushrooms simply weren't there, and my grandmother shrugged it off and went home. It gnawed on my father, though, because he wanted to know why *they weren't there. Thus began his lifelong pursuit of wild mushrooms, which has lasted to this day.*

I have often been as astounded at the absence of mushrooms as I have at their abundance. I have gone into the woods after a rain and found nothing—even though the conditions and timing were right. With gritted teeth I have many times emerged from a promising woods with nothing but my knife in the basket. Now here's something really eerie. It has happened to me only twice, but it's strange nonetheless. We also use cultivated mushrooms in the restaurant, and twice when I called suppliers for them (once for shiitake, the other time for oyster mushrooms) there were none to be found anywhere. In both cases suppliers told me that they just seemed to disappear because nobody in the country had been able to grow them. This lasted for one or two days, and then they were plentiful once again. But bear in mind that we were talking about cultivated mushrooms and nobody could grow them. Coincidence? Probably, but spooky all the same. I have also found mushrooms carpeting the forest floor in the midst of a hot and dry August. And then there have been wet summer days when the abundance and variety were astounding.

Based on these experiences, I have formed a theory that I believe is foolproof. When the angels are dancing in heaven they reach such a height of merriment that they rhythmically stomp in unison, causing thundershowers. This angels' stomp reverberates to earth, where it excites the mycelium to fruit forth with mushrooms of glorious color and number. And when the dancing stops the ground begins to settle and goes to sleep, taking the mushrooms with it back into the earth. So when we venture into the woods and find our treasures fresh and vigorous, we know the angels have stomped to the tune of thunder and shared their celebration with us.

Basic Mushroom Duxelles

Invented by the famous seventeenth-century chef La Varenne, and named for his patron, the Marquis d'Uxelles, this reduced mushroom paste remains one of the cornerstones of classic French cuisine. It has a very strong flavor and the French have found many uses for it. It can be spread on canapés, added to cream soups for instant flavor, spread on beef, game, or fowl, and even layered between sheets of puff pastry to make flavorful hors d'oeuvres. It can be frozen and keeps for months. I recommend that you make a quantity that can be pulled from your freezer as needed.

This basic recipe is made from button mushrooms. I encourage you to experiment with variations once you have made the basic recipe. I have added tomatoes, garlic, Chinese oyster sauce, fresh oysters, smoked salmon, cheese, and fresh herbs. Add these as you cook down the duxelles. Just remember to check for salt as you add them. You can also make duxelles from wild mushrooms, but remember that wild mushrooms have less water than domestic mushrooms.

One final detail—you should chop the mushrooms for duxelles by hand rather than using a food processor. Finished duxelles need some residual texture that only comes from reducing finely chopped, rather than mashed, mushrooms.

---

3 tablespoons butter

²/₃ cup chopped onion

2 cups finely chopped button mushrooms

¹/₄ teaspoon salt

¹/₄ teaspoon sugar

¹/₂ teaspoon soy sauce

Melt the butter in a medium sauté pan over medium heat. Add the onion, and sauté until it is translucent, about 3 minutes. Add the mushrooms, salt, sugar, and soy sauce and continue to stir slowly. The mushrooms will begin to give off liquid. Continue to stir the mushrooms until all the liquid has evaporated and the mixture resembles a paste, 8 to 12 minutes. Remove from the heat, let cool, and pack in a jar. Refrigerate or freeze.

Makes 1 cup

Mushrooms with Basil in Potato Sauce

Cream sauces have gotten a bad reputation in the course of our switch to lower fat cooking. I like cream sauces but realize that not everyone can tolerate them for health reasons. If you are looking for a cream sauce that uses minimal cream, try this one. Remember, however, that the sauce has body and that mushrooms prepared this way must have some lively herb-acid character to offset the richness of the sauce. Also, larger mushrooms are a little better for this dish; smaller ones can be used, but must be cooked at slightly higher heat so they do not give off too much liquid.

The sauce can be made ahead of time and reheated in the microwave; however, you may have to add some milk because the potatoes will absorb some of the moisture while sitting in the refrigerator. Also, you may need to add more cream and milk to obtain the right consistency, since some potatoes have less moisture than others.

Most food processors come with a warning about processing potatoes, but I find they work well when making a sauce. But you'll also need a blender to puree the basil properly.

---

6 small new potatoes, peeled, or
3 russet potatoes, peeled and
cut in half

1 pound fresh mushrooms,
preferably domestic buttons with
2-inch or larger caps

$^3/_4$ cup firmly packed fresh
basil leaves

1 tablespoon white wine vinegar

$^1/_4$ cup heavy cream

$^1/_4$ cup milk

Salt

2 tablespoons olive oil

Bring about 3 quarts of lightly salted water to a boil. Add the potatoes, cover, and cook until the potatoes are soft when pierced with a fork, about 30 minutes.

While the potatoes are cooking, clean the mushrooms and set aside. Place the basil, $^1/_4$ cup water, and the vinegar in a blender and process until well pureed. Transfer to a bowl and set aside.

Drain the potatoes, place in a food processor, and process until well pureed, stopping occasionally to wipe down the sides with a rubber spatula. Place the potatoes in a blender and add the cream and milk (in two batches if necessary). Then blend until the mixture is smooth, adding a little more milk, if necessary, until the mixture has the consistency of a thickened sauce rather than mashed potatoes. Pour this mixture through a medium-fine sieve to eliminate any lumps. Place the sauce in a small saucepan and reheat, stirring. Add salt to taste and keep the sauce warm.

Place the basil puree and the olive oil in a sauté pan and begin to warm over medium heat. Add the mushrooms and sauté for 5 minutes adding a little salt to taste. Evenly divide the warmed potato sauce among 4 plates, covering the plates from rim to rim. Arrange the herb-sautéed mushrooms in the middle of the sauce and serve immediately.

Variation: For a different and pretty presentation, sauté the mushrooms with some minced garlic and scallion in the oil. Prepare the basil mixture, but combine the potato sauce with the herb puree for a light green sauce to pour onto the plates. Arrange the mushrooms in the middle, over the herb-potato sauce.

Serves 4
Suggested wine: Acacia Pinot Noir

Eggs with Curried Mushrooms Sur le Plat

Simplicity is the essence of all good cooking, and this use of mushrooms is one of the most straightforward you can imagine. Any type of mushrooms can be used but be sure they are cut into bite-size pieces.

Preheat the oven to 325° F.

Place the butter and oil in a large sauté pan over medium heat. Sauté the mushrooms and scallions until the mushrooms begin to become limp, about 2 minutes. Add the curry powder, cumin, pepper, and chile, then continue to sauté until the mushrooms are well cooked, about 5 to 7 minutes. You may have to add more oil, because some mushrooms will absorb the oil more quickly than others.

Spread the mushroom mixture evenly on 4 ovenproof serving plates. Break 2 eggs onto each of the plates and place in the oven. Bake until the eggs are set, 6 to 7 minutes, then serve immediately.

Serves 4

---

2 tablespoons butter

2 tablespoons olive oil

4 ounces fresh button mushrooms, cleaned and medium sliced

2 whole scallions, thinly sliced

1/4 teaspoon curry powder

1/4 teaspoon ground cumin

Pinch of black pepper

1 teaspoon chopped serrano chile (optional)

8 eggs

Button Mushroom–Avocado Salad
with Cilantro Dressing

The deep, buttery texture of button mushrooms and the rich avocado flavors are contrasted with a tart sauce made from cilantro and a little oil. Portobellos can also be used.

This salad really must be made right before serving, because the avocado quickly oxidizes to an ugly brown once it is sliced and exposed to air.

½ cup loosely packed fresh cilantro leaves

1½ teaspoons white wine vinegar

3 tablespoons olive oil

6 ounces fresh button mushrooms or portobello caps, cleaned and sliced ½ inch thick

2 medium avocados, split, seeded, and cut to approximately the size of the mushroom slices

Mesclun greens (optional)

In a blender, combine the cilantro, 2 tablespoons water, and the vinegar and blend to a puree. Slowly add the olive oil while blending to make the dressing.

Toss together the mushrooms, avocado slices, and dressing. This salad can be served alone or on top of mesclun.

Serves 4

Grilled Beef with Mushrooms and Chile Sauce

This easy, versatile chile sauce is useful for grilled or broiled steaks. It has an intense flavor when tasted by itself, but remember that it is meant to be served with beef, which can easily overwhelm less highly seasoned sauces. Large, beefy mushrooms like portobellos go best with it.

If you are grilling the steaks, simply grill the mushroom slices along with the steaks. You can also cut the steak into cubes and skewer the meat along with the mushrooms, brushing the steaks with the sauce just before the steaks are done.

Heat a charcoal grill or broiler and prepare the steaks for grilling by removing most but not all of the fat.

In a small saucepan combine the wine, ½ cup water, the sugar, soy sauce, mustard, black pepper, coriander, and ground chiles and put over low heat. When hot, stir in the cornstarch mixture and stir until the sauce becomes slightly thickened. You do not want the sauce to become too thick. Set aside.

Begin grilling or broiling the steaks. While they are cooking, sauté the mushrooms in the oil along with the onions and peppers until the onions and peppers are somewhat limp, about 2 minutes. Remove the steaks when they are done to your liking and place one on each plate. Cover each steak with sauce and place the mushroom mixture over the steaks before serving.

---

4 filets mignons or sirloin steaks, about 8 ounces each

½ cup dry red wine

1 teaspoon sugar

2 tablespoons dark soy sauce

1 tablespoon Dijon mustard

½ teaspoon crushed black pepper

½ teaspoon ground coriander

1 teaspoon ground red chiles or chili pepper

2 teaspoons cornstarch mixed with ⅓ cup cold water

1 pound fresh portobellos, cleaned

¼ cup vegetable oil

2 large onions, thinly sliced

2 large red bell peppers, thinly sliced (optional)

Serves 4

Suggested wine: Cabernet Sauvignon or Petit Sirah

Mushroom Caps Stuffed with Spicy Guacamole

These are great for putting people in a party mood.

Combine the tomatoes, onion, chiles, and salt in a medium bowl and allow to macerate for 15 minutes.

Meanwhile, split the avocado in half and remove the seed. Scoop out the avocado meat and place in a food processor. Add the cilantro, vinegar, 2 tablespoons water, and the lemon juice and blend until smooth.

Fold the avocado puree into the tomato mixture and refrigerate for 1 hour before using.

Adjust seasoning for filling with salt if necessary. Stuff the mushroom caps with the guacamole and serve.

Serves 8 to 10
Suggested wine: Long Vineyards Sauvignon Blanc

2 medium tomatoes, seeded and diced
1 small onion, diced
2 serrano chiles, finely diced
1 teaspoon salt
1 ripe medium avocado
1/2 bunch fresh cilantro, stems removed
1 tablespoon white wine vinegar
Juice of 1 lemon
1 to 2 pounds fresh button mushrooms, cleaned and stems removed

Portobello Stems with Potatoes and Garlic

As romantic and robust as whole portobellos are, it is the caps that are used for most dishes. Generally, it is a good idea to make duxelles with the stems (see page 21), but sometimes it's just too time-consuming, or maybe you already have enough duxelles to last a lifetime. Here is another way to use extra stems. The relative amounts of mushrooms and potatoes are not really important—this is a true convenience dish that depends on your quantity of stems. This is also a handy way to use stems of fresh cèpes, which can also be quite large, and the stems of large domestic button mushrooms can be used the same way. Do not slice the stems too thin because some portobello stems are partially hollow and not uniformly dense.

Slice the potatoes into ⅛- to ¼-inch-thick rounds. Then slice the rounds again into match-stick-size pieces, ⅛- to ¼-inch-wide and about 2 to 3 inches long. Keep covered with cold water until ready to use.

Place the butter and oil in a large sauté pan. Heat over medium heat, then add the potatoes. Fry the potatoes until they begin to brown, about 4 minutes. Add the onion and garlic and continue to fry until the potatoes begin to soften, about 5 minutes more. Add the mushroom stems and continue to fry, adding more oil if the mixture is too dry. When the mush-rooms begin to go limp, in about 3 minutes, add the paprika and salt to taste. Sprinkle parsley on top and serve as a side dish.

Serves 4 as a side dish
Suggested wine: Chaddsford Pinot Rouge or a good Beaujolais

---

2 large russet potatoes, peeled

2 tablespoons butter

2 tablespoons vegetable oil, or more as needed

1 small onion, finely chopped

2 garlic cloves, finely chopped

Cleaned stems from 4 large fresh portobellos, sliced in ½ to ¾ inch rounds

Spanish paprika

Salt

1 tablespoon chopped fresh parsley

Portobellos with Watercress

Every spring as the snows melt and the earth becomes fruitful once again, a little creek across the field from my house becomes filled with the rich green tufts of fresh watercress. Although great by itself in salads, watercress also gives sauces an elegant green appearance and a spicy, sharp flavor unmatched by any other green. This is one of my favorite ways to use it.

In this recipe, you can substitute other mushrooms, but portobellos absorb the watercress flavor best. Slice the portobello stems lengthwise into quarters if you want to sauté them also. If you do, then they must be sautéed for a minute before adding the caps because they are firmer and take longer to cook.

½ cup fresh watercress, stems removed

1 tablespoon white wine vinegar

¼ cup olive oil

2 large fresh portobello caps, cleaned with stems removed and sliced ½ inch thick (see above)

Salt

Mixed green salad (optional)

Combine the watercress, ¼ cup water, and the vinegar in a blender and blend until you have a puree. Transfer to a large sauté pan along with the oil and begin to warm over medium heat. Add the mushroom caps. Lightly salt the mushrooms, and cover with a loose-fitting lid. Braise the mushrooms for 3 minutes. Remove the lid and season to taste. Serve the mushrooms by themselves or in a salad with mixed greens.

Serves 4

Suggested wine: Stag's Leap Sauvignon Blanc

Sautéed Mushrooms with Herbs

If you like mushrooms light and nutritious, with the mushroom flavor as pure as possible, this is one of the best ways to prepare them. Make an herb puree, combine with a little oil, and sauté the mushrooms in this mixture.

You may have to use varying amounts of oil and herb mixture depending on the mushroom used for this dish. Some mushrooms, like portobellos, absorb the liquid in the sauté pan very quickly; you have to add a little more so the mushrooms do not burn before they are cooked. Other varieties, like oyster mushrooms, absorb less, so you must watch carefully while you sauté them.

You may also use dried herbs for this dish. Reduce the amount of herbs to 2 tablespoons and proceed as directed.

Clean the mushrooms and remove the stems. (The stems can be also used for sautéing, but some, like shiitake, are tough and must be discarded.)

If mushroom caps are large, slice them.

In a blender or food processor, combine the vinegar, herbs, and ¼ cup water and process until smooth. (With certain herbs you may have to run the puree through a fine sieve to remove residual stem bits.)

Combine the herb mixture and oil in a large sauté pan and begin to warm over medium heat. Add the mushrooms and sauté for about 5 minutes, or until desired doneness. Add salt to taste. (*Caution:* If you are using wild mushrooms, cook them until they are thoroughly limp and tender. Domestic or exotic domestic mushrooms may be left slightly raw for texture's sake.)

Use these mushrooms as a side dish or as a course on its own, especially if you are using rare wild mushrooms.

Serves 4
Suggested wine: Matanzas Creek Sauvignon Blanc

---

12 ounces fresh wild mushrooms
1 tablespoon white wine vinegar
⅓ cup loosely packed fresh herbs, such as thyme, sage, and oregano, stems removed
3 tablespoons olive oil
Salt

Wild Mushrooms Tuscan Style

When you want to make a mushroom dish that is as unadorned as possible—free of intrusive added flavors—this is your dish: no butter, no cream, and a minimum of fuss. It works for any type of mushroom except those few that do not give off much liquid while cooking.

Place the oil in a skillet over medium heat. Add the onion and sauté until they become slightly browned, 2 or 3 minutes. Add ½ cup

2 tablespoons extra-virgin olive oil

½ cup sliced or chopped onion

8 ounces fresh button mushrooms or any variety of domestic or wild mushrooms

1 teaspoon salt

1 teaspoon sugar

1 tablespoon soy sauce

½ teaspoon dried savory

2 teaspoons cornstarch mixed with ¼ cup cold water

water, then add the mushrooms and cover the skillet. Simmer for 30 minutes. The mushrooms will greatly reduce in size and be completely covered with liquid.

Add the salt, sugar, soy sauce, and savory and stir. Simmer for another 5 minutes, then stir in the cornstarch mixture, blend until thickened, and serve.

Serves 4

Suggested wine: Chalone Chardonnay

Buttons and Black Trumpets
in Hot Sausage Sauce

Mushroom purists generally prefer not to mix mushrooms. Too bad. One of the really enjoyable aspects of mushroom cooking is combining several types to have a dish that is greater than the sum of its parts, especially if you have a limited number of wild mushrooms on hand. Let's say you go to a specialty food store to buy some exotic mushrooms and hit the roof when you find out how much they cost. Not to worry, because you can use a small amount of exotics and fill in with button mushrooms.

Other exotic or wild varieties can be substituted for the black trumpets. If you cannot locate wild mushrooms, use shiitake or even oyster mushrooms, available in most grocery stores now.

Place the oil in a large saucepan over medium heat. Add the onion and sauté for 1 minute. Add the kielbasa and chile and sauté for another minute. Add the mushrooms and sauté for 1 minute or until a little liquid is drawn from them. When you see the liquid collecting at the bottom of the saucepan, cover the pan with a tight-fitting lid, reduce the heat to low, and cook, covered, for 10 minutes.

Remove the lid from the saucepan and add the salt, basil, rosemary, tomato paste, and sugar. Stir together well and continue to simmer over low heat. The mixture should begin to thicken, becoming slightly thick without being runny. If it does not thicken sufficiently, add a little more tomato paste.

Serve as an appetizer, a vegetable dish, or as an accompaniment to game, fowl, or rabbit. If served as an appetizer, accompany with pasta or bulgur.

---

3 tablespoons vegetable oil

1 small onion, chopped

4 ounces kielbasa (Polish sausage), finely chopped

1 serrano chile, finely chopped, or 2 or 3 if you really like it hot

1 pound fresh button mushrooms, thickly sliced (in only 2 or 3 slices), stems on

4 ounces fresh black trumpets (Craterellus fallax) or other wild mushrooms

2 teaspoons salt

1 tablespoon finely chopped fresh basil

1 tablespoon finely chopped fresh rosemary

3 tablespoons tomato paste, or more as needed

1 teaspoon sugar

Serves 4
Suggested wine: Guigal Rhone or Guenoc Petit Sirah

Swordfish with a Plum-Mushroom Topping

The thick sauce here is made from duxelles with the simple addition of flour and egg to set the mixture so it layers evenly over the fish. But be sure to spread the sauce evenly over the fish before cooking because the fish's tapered ends tend to dry and get too crusty.

Preheat the oven to 425° F.

Beat the egg in a small bowl. Add the flour and beat until smooth. Add the duxelles and blend well.

Place each filet in the middle of a piece of parchment paper or aluminum foil. Spread the mixture evenly over the surface of each filet, using all of the mixture. Sprinkle a little oil evenly over the mixture, then close the parchment by folding the 3 sides over and stapling shut. (If using aluminum foil, simply fold the edges together to close so that the fish is completely enclosed.) Place the filets on a baking sheet and bake for 10 minutes. Remove from the oven and serve immediately.

Serves 4

Suggested wine: Mirassou Pinot Blanc

> *1 egg*
> *1 tablespoon flour*
> *4 tablespoons Plum-Mushroom Duxelles (page 36)*
> *4 swordfish filets, about 6 ounces each*
> *Vegetable oil*

Painted Portobellos in Puff Pastry

If you like appetizers that are quick, easy, and delicious, this is for you. The "paint" here can be anything from hoisin sauce to a ready-made Mexican mole, or any combination of thick sauces such as oyster or black bean. I like spicy food, so I use the following combination for this dish. Use a blender to puree the chipotle peppers.

This dish can also be made with any of the larger wild mushrooms and is especially good with larger boletes. Just avoid using especially delicate mushrooms, such as the oyster mushroom.

Preheat the oven to 425° F.

Roll out the puff pastry on a floured surface so that it can be easily folded over the caps. Since portobello caps vary in size, you may have to roll out the puff pastry to different sizes.

Paint the caps and undersides of the mushrooms liberally with the puree and place cap down on the puff pastry. Fold the puff pastry ends up so they meet and completely enclose each mushroom cap. Turn the pastry packages over and place on a lined baking sheet. Brush some egg wash over each puff pastry package and then cut a decorative design into the pastry if you wish.

Place in the oven and bake for 7 minutes, or until the pastry is golden. Serve immediately.

Serves 4

Suggested wine: Parker Riesling

---

4 5-inch squares all-butter puff pastry (available frozen in grocery stores)

4 fresh portobellos, 3 to 5 inches wide (no wider), cleaned and stems removed

2 tablespoons pureed chipotle peppers in adobo sauce, blended with 2 tablespoons Chinese oyster sauce

1 egg, lightly beaten with 1 tablespoon water

Plum-Mushroom Duxelles

You might not think of fruit with mushrooms as an appealing combination. And, in fact, most fruit does not work well with mushrooms, but plums are an exception. The key here is that plums are often not as sweet as many other fruits and they possess a tangy, tannic skin that makes them seem less sweet than they are. So remember—don't peel the plums!

Although Plum-Mushroom Duxelles can be made with whole mushrooms, it offers a great way to use up mushroom stems. Use this duxelles in dishes made with duck, scallops, or a rich, oily fish such as mackerel or shad.

> *3 tablespoons butter*
> *⅔ cup chopped onion*
> *2 cups chopped fresh button mushrooms (about 8 ounces)*
> *½ teaspoon salt*
> *½ teaspoon soy sauce*
> *1 small prune plum, pitted and chopped, with skin left on*

Melt the butter in a large sauté pan over medium heat and add the onion. Sauté for 1 minute, then add the mushrooms. Continue to sauté; the mushrooms will begin to release their liquid and the mixture will be very wet for a few minutes until the liquid begins to evaporate. As the mixture begins to dry out, in about 5 minutes, add the salt and soy sauce. Finally add the plum and sauté for another 2 minutes.

The duxelles can be kept for about a week in the refrigerator or frozen for several months.

Makes 1 cup

Portobello Pizza

Elements of Mexican and Asian cuisines combine to make this one of my favorite ways to prepare portobellos. For this "pizza," the mushroom cap becomes the crust. If you do not like spicy foods, you can omit the chipotle chiles and paint the mushrooms with oyster sauce, using a little more than indicated below.

Preheat the oven to 400° F.

Cut the stems off the portobellos and use for another purpose, such as duxelles. Clean the caps with a wet cloth.

Puree the chipotles and oyster sauce in a blender until smooth; add a little water if necessary. Set aside.

Heat the oil over medium heat in a large sauté pan. Sauté the onion and poblanos until the mixture begins to wilt, then add some salt. The mixture should be somewhat moist rather than dry because the onion and chiles can dry out while in the oven.

4 fresh portobellos, 3 to 5 inches wide

3 canned chipotle chiles in adobo sauce

2 tablespoons oyster sauce

1/3 cup vegetable oil

1 large red onion, sliced

3 poblano chiles or green bell peppers, sliced

Salt

4 ounces Mexican Chihuahua or other good melting cheese such as Monterey Jack, grated or sliced

Continue to sauté for 3 minutes, then remove from heat and let cool to room temperature.

Paint the bottoms of the mushrooms with the chipotle–oyster sauce mixture. With the caps bottom side up, distribute the onion-poblano mixture over the tops of the mushrooms.

Place the mushrooms on a lined baking sheet and bake for 5 minutes. Remove and spread the cheese over the tops, then return the mushrooms to the oven and bake for another minute, or until all the cheese is melted. Serve immediately.

Note: Canned chipotle chiles are available in Mexican grocery stores or in the ethnic sections of large supermarkets. Oyster sauce is available in Asian grocery stores.

Serves 4
Suggested wine: Ridge Petit Sirah

Trestled Swordfish with Mushrooms and Dried Oyster Sauce

The trestles in this dish are simmered mushrooms used to prop up the swordfish filet. You can use four mushrooms of the same height, six or seven very small mushrooms, or even several mushrooms of different heights, starting with the smallest at one end and the highest at the other so that the filet is angled upward off the plate according to the position of the mushrooms.

Preheat the oven to 350° F.

In a 2-quart saucepan, combine the oysters, 4 cups water, the soy sauce, sesame oil, and wine. Bring to a brisk boil over high heat and then turn down to a simmer. Simmer for 20 minutes.

While the liquid is simmering, trim the stems of the mushrooms so that they can stand up on their own. Add the mushrooms to the liquid and simmer for 5 minutes. Remove the mushrooms from the liquid and keep warm.

Place the swordfish in a roasting pan and bake for 10 minutes.

In a small sauté pan, combine the flour and butter and stir over medium heat until light golden or even slightly brown.

Remove the oysters from the liquid and discard. Whisk the flour mixture into the liquid and continue to stir until the flour is completely incorporated into the liquid. Place over medium-low heat and continue to stir the liquid slowly until the sauce thickens. It should coat a spoon and be reddish brown. Remove the sauce from the heat. There should be 2 to 2½ cups of sauce.

Coat 4 dinner plates with some of the sauce. Place 4 to 5 caps standing up and in line in the sauce. Place a fish filet over each trestle and serve immediately, with additional sauce on the side.

Variation: If you'd prefer, you can grill the swordfish over charcoal for 2 minutes on each side. Also, shark can be substituted for the swordfish.

Serves 4

Suggested wine: Chaddsford Cabernet Sauvignon

½ cup dried oysters (available in Asian markets)

½ cup soy sauce

1 teaspoon roasted sesame oil

1 cup dry red wine

16 to 20 fresh button or cremini mushrooms, brushed clean and quickly rinsed

4 long-cut filets of swordfish, 6 to 8 ounces each

3 tablespoons flour

3 tablespoons butter, melted

Heidi's Potatoes with Portobellos

I have a lot of fun coming up with new recipes. The process usually starts with some concept of what I'm trying to do, followed by trial and error in the kitchen, eventually resulting in a finished recipe. My wife, Heidi, on the other hand, seems to wave her magic wand around the kitchen and come up with devastatingly wonderful dishes with seemingly nothing but intuition to guide her. Each of her inspirations humbles me a bit more. This recipe is an example of why she is a much better cook than I am.

Potatoes with Portobellos can be served as part of a larger meal or as an entree.

Preheat the oven to 425° F.

Place the potatoes in a pot of lightly salted water. Bring to a boil and cook until very tender when pierced with a fork, but not until the potatoes fall apart when pierced, about 30 minutes.

While the potatoes are cooking, place 3 tablespoons of the oil in a skillet over medium heat. Add 1 tablespoon of the garlic and sauté for 1 minute. Add the spinach and stir until it begins to wilt. When the spinach is fully wilted, add salt to taste. Spread the sautéed spinach over the bottom of a 12-inch glass baking dish.

Remove the stems from the mushrooms and cut

---

3 to 4 medium new potatoes, preferably red

5 tablespoons olive oil

2 tablespoons minced garlic

10 ounces fresh spinach

Salt

2 large fresh portobellos, cleaned

6 ounces Boursin cheese, or any other herbed cream cheese

---

the caps into ½-inch pieces. Then slice the stems into ½-inch-wide pieces. Add the remaining oil and garlic to the skillet and sauté for 1 minute. Add the sliced mushroom stems and caps and sauté over medium-high heat. Some liquid will be released from the mushrooms. Sauté until most of the liquid has evaporated and the mushrooms have turned nearly black, about 4 minutes. Add salt to taste.

When the potatoes are tender, remove them from the water and slice into ½-inch-thick pieces while still warm. Layer the potatoes over the spinach and lightly salt this layer.

Layer the mushrooms over the potatoes. Break up the cheese as much as possible and scatter over the mushrooms.

Place the dish, uncovered, in the oven and bake for 20 minutes. Remove the dish and spread the cheese carefully over the mushrooms with a spatula. This is not really a melting cheese, so you must spread it when you remove it warm from the oven. Serve immediately.

Serves 4
Suggested wine: Woodward Canyon Cabernet Sauvignon

Scallops with Oyster Duxelles and Mushroom-Sage Sauce

The metallic sweetness of Chinese oyster sauce is the perfect counterpoint to the earthy mushroom flavor of the duxelles. Choose the largest, most succulent scallops you can find for this dish, which you can serve as a main course with a walnut and curry rice.

Put 1 tablespoon of the butter in a medium skillet, set over medium heat, and add the onion. Sauté for 1 minute, then add the mushrooms and continue to sauté. They will begin to release their liquid. Sauté until the liquid is all but completely evaporated, about 5 minutes.

Stir in the oysters, oyster sauce, and sage, and heat, stirring until the ingredients are well blended. Set duxelles aside and keep warm.

In a large skillet, add the oil and remaining butter and place over medium heat. When slightly smoking, add the scallops and sauté for 2 to 3 minutes on each side or until just rare in the middle but browned on the outside. Remove from the skillet.

Add the cream to the skillet along with the lemon juice and heat, stirring, until the sauce begins to thicken. Add salt to taste, then remove from the heat.

Mound the duxelles in the middle of 4 individual plates. Place 4 scallops around the duxelles on each plate and spoon the sauce onto the scallops, about 1 teaspoon per scallop.

2 tablespoons butter
2 tablespoons chopped onion
3/4 cup chopped fresh mushrooms
2 tablespoons chopped raw oysters
1 teaspoon Chinese oyster sauce
1 teaspoon finely chopped fresh sage
1 tablespoon vegetable oil
16 large sea scallops, lightly salted
1/3 cup heavy cream
Juice of 1 lemon
Salt

Serves 4
Suggested wine: Chaddsford Stargazer Chardonnay

Pennsylvania Pasta with Cremini

Egg noodles are the heart and soul of Pennsylvania Dutch cooking. They are not as prevalent as pasta is in the Italian kitchen, but that is because the Pennsylvania Dutch have an equal fondness for potatoes. Egg noodles are almost always served as a side dish with meat, but can be used as universally as their pasta cousins.

Melt the butter in a skillet and add the onion. Sauté over medium-high heat until the onion is just translucent, 1 to 2 minutes. Stop the cooking by adding ½ cup water to the skillet. Stir in the seasonings, lemon juice, wine, sugar, and soy sauce. Add the mushrooms and turn the heat to low. Cover the skillet with a tight-fitting lid and simmer for 30 minutes.

Meanwhile, bring a pot of lightly salted water (about 4 quarts) to a boil. Add the noodles and cook until just slightly firm. Drain.

While the noodles are cooking, stir the cornstarch mixture into the mushrooms and heat until thickened. Place the noodles on a serving dish and spoon the mushrooms and sauce over. This dish can be reheated very successfully.

---

3 tablespoons butter
½ cup chopped onion
½ teaspoon ground coriander
½ teaspoon chili powder
1 teaspoon minced garlic
¼ teaspoon black pepper
1 teaspoon salt
1 teaspoon lemon juice
¼ cup dry red wine
1 teaspoon sugar
1 tablespoon soy sauce
½ pound fresh cremini, sliced
5 ounces dried egg noodles
1½ tablespoons cornstarch, mixed with ⅓ cup cold water

Serves 4

Suggested wine: Allegro Pennsylvania Cabernet Sauvignon

See photograph on page 2

Curried Mushroom Soup

A fresh mushroom sitting on the grocer's shelf looks pretty substantial, but is mostly water encased in more solid cellular material. That is why mushrooms really make their own soup when you heat them up. Their liquid is released upon cooking, thereby coating, then covering, the remaining solid flesh of the mushroom. So, when using fresh mushrooms, you really don't need to add too much more liquid to make a soup. As an extra bonus, the liquid trapped inside is redolent of the mushroom's savory and aromatic features. That is the underlying technique in this recipe—just let the mushroom do its thing. Also, by pureeing the stems you thicken the soup without the traditional helpers— such as cornstarch or flour.

Any of the domestic relatives of button mushrooms can also be used, portobello or cremini, for example.

Separate the stems and caps of the mushrooms. Set stems aside. Place ¼ cup water in a small sauce-

2 pounds fresh domestic button mushrooms, preferably small caps (if using portobellos, slice into ½-inch pieces, then cut again into thirds)

1 medium onion, thinly sliced

2 tablespoons soy sauce

2 cups half-and-half

1 tablespoon curry powder

¼ teaspoon sugar

1 teaspoon Spanish paprika

1 tablespoon white wine vinegar

Heavy cream

Salt

Crème fraîche or sour cream

pan over high heat and add the mushroom caps. Bring the water to a boil, then lower to a simmer, add the onion, and cover with a tight-fitting lid. The mushrooms will release their liquid and shrink as they "sweat," from 5 to 7 minutes.

While the caps are cooking, combine the soy sauce, mushroom stems, ⅓ cup half-and-half, curry powder, sugar, paprika, and vinegar in a blender or food processor and process until you have a smooth, fairly thick puree.

Place the puree and mushrooms in a soup pot, along with the remaining half-and-half, adding just enough cream until you have your desired thickness. Heat until warmed through, and season with salt to taste. Ladle into individual soup bowls and add a dollop of crème fraîche or sour cream just before serving.

Serves 4

Wild Mushrooms in Harlequin Sauce

This is a versatile way to cook any kind of wild mushrooms. It can be served on its own or used as a sauce for chicken, pork, veal, or game birds.

Place the fresh mushrooms in a large saucepan and add ½ cup water. Bring to a boil over high heat, then reduce heat, cover with a tight-fitting lid, and let the mushrooms "sweat" for 20 minutes.

Pour the liquid from the mushrooms into a small saucepan, leaving the fresh mushrooms in the large pan. Set mushrooms aside.

Add the dried cèpes to the small saucepan and bring to a boil over high heat. Reduce the heat

to low and simmer the cèpes in this liquid for 20 minutes or until very soft. Place the cèpes and ½ cup of the liquid in a blender. (If there's not enough cooking liquid, add a little water.) Puree until smooth.

Return the mushroom puree to the saucepan and add the butter, tomato paste, cream, wine, basil, sage, sugar, and salt. Simmer over medium heat until slightly thickened, about 5 minutes. Strain the sauce, then add to the sweated fresh mushrooms. Reheat and serve.

1 pound fresh wild mushrooms
¼ ounce dried cèpes
2 tablespoons butter
1 tablespoon tomato paste
1 cup heavy cream
¼ cup dry white wine
1 tablespoon chopped fresh basil
or 1 teaspoon dried
1 teaspoon dried sage
½ teaspoon sugar
½ teaspoon salt

Serves 4
Suggested wine: Robert Mueller Chardonnay

Breakfast Portobellos with Shiitake

There are many variations on this theme, using different mushrooms in one dish. This breakfast preparation can be embellished with melted cheese and bacon. Any large-capped wild mushrooms can be used.

Preheat the oven to 400° F.

Place the portobello caps, gill side up, in a large baking dish and bake for 5 minutes.

While the mushrooms are baking, heat the oil in a large sauté pan over high heat. Add the shiitakes, onion, and corn, then sauté until the mushrooms are limp and the corn is tender, about 3 to 4 minutes. Add the pine nuts and bacon, and stir well. Season with salt to taste, bearing in mind that the mixture will be going on top of the portobellos. Be sure to season it well, even make it a little salty.

---

4 medium to large fresh portobello caps, 4 to 6 inches, cleaned

3 tablespoons olive oil

4 ounces fresh shiitakes, stems removed and caps sliced

1/2 small onion, finely diced

1 cup fresh corn kernels

1/3 cup toasted pine nuts

1/2 cup crumbled bacon (optional)

Salt

8 eggs

Remove the mushrooms from the oven and evenly divide the shiitake mixture among the 4 caps, smoothing the surfaces. Make sure the caps lay as flat as possible in the baking dish so that the eggs will not slide to one side while baking. Crack 2 eggs over the top of each mushroom. Lightly salt the eggs and return the dish to the oven. Bake until the eggs are done, then serve at once.

Variation: Add a few strips of a good melting cheese over each cap just as the eggs begin to set, then return them to the oven until the cheese has melted.

Serves 4

Button Mushrooms in Coconut Milk

There is something exciting about food cooked in coconut milk. Typically, the effect comes from the addition of several assertive spices—such as coriander, cumin, and cardamom—in conjunction with this rich liquid. In Indian cuisine, ginger and hot peppers are frequently added to give zest and dimension.

Although this recipe is for mushrooms only, you can make this a heftier dish by adding scallops or shrimp. Simply simmer them for a minute or two in the sauce while it is thickening.

You can make this a day ahead and reheat it. The flavors have a better chance to blend that way, and the mixture will become thicker.

Place the shredded coconut and 4 cups of water in a 2-quart saucepan. Put over high heat and bring to a boil. Reduce the heat and simmer for 15 minutes. Remove saucepan from the heat and place contents in a food processor or blender. Process for 1 full minute, then strain the milk through a fine sieve, squeezing out as much liquid as possible. There should be about 3 cups of coconut milk. Set aside.

1 (14-ounce) package unsweetened shredded coconut (see Note)

⅓ cup vegetable oil

3 large onions, finely chopped

1 tablespoon minced garlic

4 ounces fresh ginger, peeled and finely chopped

Hot chiles of your choice, such as 2 jalapeños or 4 serranos

½ teaspoon curry powder

1 tablespoon ground coriander

1 tablespoon ground cardamom

1 tablespoon ground cumin

1 pound small fresh button mushrooms (or any other variety)

Salt

2 tablespoons finely chopped fresh cilantro

Cooked basmati rice

Place the oil in a large saucepan over high heat. Add the onions and sauté until they begin to brown, about 2 to 3 minutes. Add the garlic, ginger, and chiles, and sauté for another minute. Add the curry, coriander, cardamom, and cumin and stir for another minute. Add the mushrooms and the coconut milk and stir well to incorporate any spices that have settled on the bottom of the pan. Simmer for 15 minutes. The mushrooms will give off their liquid and the water will begin to evaporate, then the mixture will begin to thicken. Remove from the heat when thickened. Season to taste and add the cilantro. Serve over rice.

Note: Shredded coconut is available in supermarkets. Buy the unsweetened variety if possible. If you use the sweetened variety, be mindful that the dish will taste sweeter, and this is not to everyone's liking.

Canned unsweetened coconut milk may be substituted and is available in Asian markets.

Serves 4

Suggested wine: Gewürztraminer or Riesling

Joe's Restaurant Cheesesteaks

For a cold winter's night treat, Joe's Cheesesteaks cannot be beat. Enjoy them with scalloped potatoes and close friends.

Prepare a covered charcoal grill.

Score each steak through the fat on the edge about 2 inches apart.

Place a little oil in a large skillet over high heat. Add the onions and sauté until thoroughly wilted, about 2 minutes. Salt lightly to taste, then set aside.

Grill the steaks. When they are 2 to 3 minutes short of desired doneness, top with the onions and sliced mushrooms. Add the cheese. Close the top

4 sirloin steaks, 8 ounces each
Vegetable oil
2 large onions, thinly sliced
Salt
2 large fresh portobello caps, stems removed and sliced lengthwise into 3 pieces, caps sliced 1/4 inch thick
8 ounces Roquefort, blue, or Gorgonzola cheese, crumbled with a fork

of the grill and continue to cook until the cheese is melted, another 3 to 4 minutes.

Note: If you don't want to wait until warm weather to make these steaks, sear the steaks in a skillet, then top with mushrooms, onions, and cheese and finish in a preheated 400° F. oven. For medium-rare, roast for 6 to 10 minutes; for well-done steaks, cook longer in the skillet before placing in the oven. Or you can use the broiler.

Serves 4

Suggested wine: Storybook Mountain Zinfandel

Grilled Portobellos

You can use this recipe for any of the larger wild mushrooms, with the exception of those that do not absorb liquid well, such as sulfur shelf mushrooms (Laetiporus sulphureus).

Cut the stems from the caps of the mushrooms. Slice each stem in half lengthwise.

Combine the olive oil, vinegar, soy sauce, sugar, and herbs in a bowl and blend well with a whisk. Let the marinade sit for 30 minutes if fresh herbs are used, or for 1 hour, until the dried herbs soften.

Prepare a charcoal grill or preheat the broiler.

---

3 to 4 large portobellos
1 cup olive oil
1 cup red or white wine vinegar
2 tablespoons soy sauce
1 tablespoon sugar
1/2 cup finely chopped fresh herbs, such as savory, thyme, oregano, or basil, or 1 tablespoon dried savory

---

Place the mushroom caps and sliced stems in a shallow dish and pour the marinade over. Let the mushrooms marinate for up to 10 minutes, turning occasionally to ensure uniform coating.

Remove the mushrooms from the marinade and place on the hot grill or in broiler. Grill on each side for about 2 minutes. Remove from the grill, slice caps, and serve immediately.

Serves 4

Suggested wine: Dry Creek Sauvignon Blanc

It looked like the last remnants of fallen snow—white patches here and there in a random pattern as far as the eye could see in that dark August forest. I remember it as if it were yesterday, kneeling and plucking this strange and delicate mushroom and placing cluster after cluster into my basket. I didn't even want to separate the clusters or clean the dirt off, as if that would banish the magic and make them all disappear as if it was a dream. I had never seen any Clitopilus prunulis *before—much less in this quantity—but in that year in that forest they were spread out before me like manna. I have returned to that forest every year since and been graced with an occasional single specimen here and there, as if I were being shown mercy by a higher power, who would nonetheless never allow me more than one vision of this mushroom in all its glory.*

That's the way it is sometimes. I remember similar instances when other mushrooms got their one chance to get a jump on their fungal cousins as the result of some subterranean competition. Another trip one spring is memorable for its abundance of Leucopaxxillus gigantea, *another fairly rare mushroom in eastern Pennsylvania. That year, we found hundreds of them at a time when the forests are usually quiet, with the soil flicking no more than scattered species of smaller versions up into the open. We reveled in our good fortune, but it was the only time in my life that we picked that mushroom in that quantity. Yet every time I go into a spring forest, an image of those mushrooms coating the ground flashes into my brain. Just the memory of that glorious year is enough to get me into the woods when I know there probably is nothing there.*

Morel

ARISTOCRATS OF THE FOREST

Morels and Truffles

Morels and Truffles Have Something

in common that you might not expect. Besides being two of the most recognizable and sought-after fungi for the kitchen, they share a trait that only enhances their image as the patricians of the forest; namely, they are part of a taxonomic group not considered to be mushrooms at all. In the case of truffles, this is not hard to see because they grow underground, have no distinct cap and stem, and possess aromas not even remotely similar to other mushrooms. But what about morels? They have a distinct cap and stem and look like mushrooms. There is no doubt that both morels and truffles belong to the group of fungi, but they are not mushrooms in a strict scientific sense. Mushrooms are generally from a class of fungi known as Basidiomycetes—fungi whose spores (primary reproductive bodies) are produced by structures called basidia, which resemble clubs. Morels and truffles are in a different class, known as Ascomycetes, which are characterized by spores that form inside the reproductive bodies, called asci. This may seem like small stuff to the casual reader, but to taxonomists it is like the difference between mosquitoes and lions. (I must note, however, that the Basidiomycetes themselves contain some pretty strange-looking characters like stinkhorns and earth stars, not to mention jelly fungi and coral fungi.)

Both morels and truffles are at the top of the list—some would say alone there—of favorite mushrooms for the table. Both grow under conditions unusual in the wild to say the least. In eastern Pennsylvania, morels can appear when there is little else popping up. Aristocrats they are, whether mushroom or not, and their characteristics certainly set them apart from the rest of the fungal world.

Morels

It's near the end of the third week of April in Berks County, Pennsylvania. It has rained off and on for the past several days and the temperature is climbing into the nineties, unseasonably warm for this time of year. I get into my car with Stefan, our teenage son, and we park at the base of a small hill covered with a forest of dying elms. Our baskets are ready, each with a knife sitting on the bottom. We have come to this spot before—many times before—over the last ten years. When we first discovered it, we returned home with several baskets of morels, some six inches tall and still fresh and meaty. I remember kneeling in the forest to pick the first morel, then glancing up and seeing a row of seven or eight more, each one bigger and more beautiful than the one before it. I heard myself breathing as I crawled to each one and gently detached it from its base with my knife. This day in April is the first time since then that conditions have been exactly the same. We had found a few morels here and there in the intervening years, but nothing like that treasure trove. The weather had been either too cold or too dry, or just not humid enough for them to pop. A mushroom hunter waits for years for conditions as we have this morning. Alas, this trip yields only a child's handful of morels. Stefan, stalking closer to the forest floor, has better luck than I.

There is something special about morel hunting. Maybe it's because in eastern Pennsylvania the morel is the first important mushroom of the season to appear. After the biting cold and snow of winter, the earth warms and its bed is moist, bringing forth color and beauty to feed the senses. This is more than mushroom picking; it is resurrection.

And so it is that spring begins here in Berks County. The only other fungus to appear this early is the Dryad's saddle *(Polyporus squamosus),* which can grow to heroic proportions but is usually tough and bitter, though popular in Asia. For us, morels are the only game worth pursuing, and the fact that they are scarce in most years does not deter us in the least from trying to find them. For even a small handful provides a satisfaction unmatched by few other mushrooms.

Yet for all the reverence accorded to morels, they deserve to be called the clown prince of the fungal world. It's true that they are maddeningly elusive, but they also sometimes appear in such astonishing places that one might begin to think it's a trick being played by higher powers. For instance, why could it be that some of the largest hauls of morels have been from forests that have recently experienced devastating fires? What was it about the eruption of Mount St. Helen's that produced legendary quantities of morels — ash-covered and all — the following year? Paul Stamets, the most renowned and accomplished person in the field of mushroom cultivation in the United States, has countless stories of other curious places where morels have been found, including a sludge pile around a Washington State pulp company; a rain-soaked, decomposing bale of straw in the middle of a wheat field, where an enormous morel weighing several pounds was found; the basement coal bin of a house destroyed by fire in Idaho; pots holding phlox plants at a nursery; the ashes of an indoor fireplace; and a backyard hibachi.

Additionally, I have seen morels spring up in newly scattered wood chips where landscaping had recently been done. Black morels will come up in this sort of environment, but usually just once and then be gone forever. Yet there are spots to which I return each year and find at least a few morels — mostly woods populated by elms, usually dying. I go every year to an old quarry, and even though the general area yields a few morels, they are never in the same spot!

And so it is. Once picked and tasted, morels are forever longed for. They sow spiritual spores in our psyche and in the spring we humans are summoned. We follow. There is no other explanation.

I went morel searching in Virginia a couple of years ago with my friend Paul O'Dowd, who is an avid morel hunter. Paul was general manager of the Homestead in Virginia, and he thought it would be a good idea for me to take a group of customers on the hunt into the woods and hills around the hotel. Afterwards, I would prepare a lunch with the day's catch.

We set out early, and after two hours of fruitless hunting we all sat down, exhausted and disappointed, for a short rest before we returned. Suddenly I sensed that something was wrong. The "down there and back" wasn't where it was supposed to be. I was lost. I needed some time to retrace my steps and get my bearings, so I stood up and, with a straight face, told the group of twenty or so would-be morel finders that morel hunting takes patience, that sometimes it's just a matter of getting one's eyes adjusted to the forest floor to be able to discern mushrooms growing there. So I exhorted them all to give it one last shot while I reconnoitered the hill to try to get us back to civilization. While traversing the ridge, frantically trying to find some landmarks, I heard a shout from one of the group. "Here's one, I think," she yelled. Sure enough, in the palm of her hand lay a dull, black three-inch-tall morel for all to admire. I could feel the charge of determination that sparked through the forest as the rest of the group searched the forest floor once more. Soon there were more shouts, and in twenty minutes everyone had found at least a dozen morels, except myself—who was happy to find the way home.

Now the interesting thing about this story is that the area where the group found the morels was on the same slope we had been for the previous two hours. The morels hadn't popped out; they were there all along. It was the perception of the hunters that had altered, so that they could now find the mushrooms that had been eluding them all morning. This is a familiar story. Black morels are especially devilish mushrooms to find, but the interesting part is how we alter our perceptions to find them. Skepticism turns to faith because one person finds a specimen.

At the very least, the lesson here is that perception determines experience and translates into the tangible. The objective truth in this case was the presence of morels, but the reality of picking them and taking them home was determined by a perception that was sharpened and transformed during a morning of frustration. If the idealist philosopher Bishop Berkeley had been a mycologist, he might have asked, "If a morel grows in the forest and no one finds it, does it exist?" This is an example of what mushroom hunters think about as they trudge through a forest before finding any mushrooms.

The Character and Availability of Morels

For all the excitement they elicit, there are relatively few species of morels overall. They are distinguished from other mushrooms by the honeycombed involutions in their caps. Another unique characteristic of morels is that they are hollow inside, which makes them perfect for stuffing. It's a good idea to blanch the fresh morels, then let them cool before stuffing them. (If you stuff unblanched morels, they will lose a lot of liquid when they are cooked.) After you blanch them, just prepare a good mousse stuffing, put it in a pastry bag, fit one of the narrower tips on the end, and you are ready to stuff. You can also slit the morels in half lengthwise and stuff each half, but I far prefer to stuff the whole morel so that it retains the shape of a fresh morel.

Morels have an earthy flavor that reminds me of sweet peppers and caraway, which is why I often use these ingredients when cooking morels. Other ingredients, such as garlic and herbs, are good with morels but do not enhance the natural flavor. Morels are naturally a bit chewy, especially mature specimens. Longer cooking does not necessarily tenderize them, but they do need to braise a little longer than other mushrooms, 5 to 10 minutes. The stems are always tougher than the caps, so you should buy morels with trimmed stems if possible. You have to be careful about this because larger morels (and I mean *really* large ones—six ounces or more apiece) can be more than half stem and should not demand the price of smaller ones with proportionally more cap. Also, do not be put off if the mushrooms you buy are drying around the edges—that is normal and far better than having mushrooms covered with too much moisture.

If you are lucky enough to pick a large quantity of fresh morels, be sure to get them refrigerated or dried as soon as possible. A bundle of morels left in a large bag or basket will start to rot from the inside out, so you may not realize the loss until it is too late. The heat generated within the bundle will hasten the natural enzymatic breakdown and cause rot, as it will for all mushrooms.

Dried morels are available year-round at specialty food stores. They make excellent soups and sauces because they reconstitute better than most other dried mushrooms, but remember that most of the flavor is in the soaking liquid. Dried morels can be quite expensive, but they are worth it. Be aware that dried morels from Europe can have a very different character from dried domestic morels. This is partly because European ones are usually black morels and the domestics are usually yellow or tan. The other reason is that European morels are often dried over smoke, so they have a distinctly smoky smell and flavor. Often, too, the morels have come from Pakistan and India by way of Europe, where they are simply packaged. And many morels now are picked in Mexico, where French importers buy the rights to pick the mushrooms, ship them back to France to be packaged, and thence ship them on to other parts of the world, including the United States. These smoky European morels are beguiling and

I enjoy cooking with them, but that does not mean that the domestic ones are inferior. They are just different. If you buy a quantity of dried morels and do not plan to use them in the near future, you should freeze them because freezing prevents deterioration.

You will find that whether you use fresh or dried morels, they have a proclivity for hosting larvae or insects, which become evident once you start boiling or braising the mushrooms. Thorough rinsing can alleviate this problem, it cannot solve it. As the mushrooms cook, just be ready to lift the intruders out of the water with a small sieve or spoon.

Varieties of Morels

Morel taxonomy is fairly straightforward and there are really not that many varieties. However, things do get a little complicated with black morels. All true morels are of the genus *Morchella.* Similar-looking fungi of various other genera, such as *Gyromitra* and *Verpa,* should never be confused with morels because some of them are poisonous.

Unlike the other mushrooms in this book, I have categorized the morels according to their common names, not their scientific ones. This reverse arrangement is more in keeping with the way morels are generally viewed, and avoids the taxonomic confusion that sometimes occurs with black morels.

One of the most exciting developments in recent years has been the successful domestication of morels, specifically *Morchella esculenta,* the yellow (or tan) morel. A company called Morel Mountain began selling the domesticated product several years ago to restaurants and wholesalers. In 1994, Morel Mountain was purchased by Dean Terry of Terry Farms in Mason, Minnesota, who is in the process of completing a massive new facility that will enable them to grow and sell several thousand pounds of fresh morels a week, year-round! The flavor of cultivated morels tends to be less intense than the wild ones; some people prefer them.

Half-free Morel   Scientific name—*Morchella semilibera.* This is usually the first morel in spring, although there are years when it does not appear at all. It is considered the least desirable of morels because it consists almost entirely of a long stem with just a bit of a cap, but is picked enthusiastically nonetheless because it is the first morel to appear and its presence usually promises bigger and better things to come!

Black Morel (Peck's morel)   Scientific name—*Morchella angusticeps, M. elata* (fat-headed black morel), *M. conica* (narrow-headed black morel). The first morels to appear in the latter weeks of April, these immediately follow or sometimes co-exist with half-free morels. Black morels are usually considered as separate species in a group, even though some mycologists say there is no taxonomic difference of substance or importance. These are the morels you are most likely to find in newly mulched areas of your garden or at burn sites. They are, without doubt, the toughest morel to "see" in the woods.

Yellow Morel (tan morel, honeycomb mushroom, corn cob mushroom) Scientific name—*Morchella esculenta, M. crassipes* (club-foot morel, a larger version, sometimes differentiated from *M. esculenta,* sometimes not). These are considered to be the morel lover's idea of nirvana. The yellow morel can grow quite large and enjoys a wider habitat than the black morel. Because of its color and size, it is fairly easy to spot in the woods once you have adjusted your eyes. A full basket of yellow morels is one of the prettiest sights you can imagine on this planet.

White Morel Scientific name—*Morchella deliciosa.* These small, white morels are smaller than the other morels and have a more delicate appearance but give away nothing in flavor. Their habitat is similar to that of *M. esculenta* with which it can grow side by side.

False Morels Scientific name—*Gyromitra* species. These look like morels that somebody has stepped on. Heavily involuted as are morels, they lack the regular profile of a true morel, more like some gnomes. *Gyromitra esculenta* is considered one of the most dangerous, but any field guide will tell you that it is eaten regularly in Europe, where the mushrooms are boiled several times, with water discarded each time. When eaten raw, even in Europe, they have been responsible for numerous poisonings. In any case, it's best to avoid them.

Truffles

Dubbed "Black Diamonds" by French gastronome Brillat-Savarin, the black truffles of Perigord are considered the headiest and most profound culinary treasures on the face of the earth. The Italians are equally passionate about their white truffles, found primarily in the area around Piedmont.

But why?

If you haven't smelled or tasted a truffle, it is difficult to convey the experience. The sense of smell can transport a person back into the past when a similar smell was experienced, evoking a flood of images and emotions. Truffles have the same ability to transport us into a world of sensuality. Even with its ephemeral olfactory allure, the truffle brings a phantasmal quality. Attempts to capture the haunting scent of this earth-encrusted denizen have been many. The French store truffles in raw rice or with eggs, so that the aroma permeates them and can be enjoyed even if the fungus is not present.

The truffle character is often associated with sex. Indeed, it is said people respond to truffles much the way they respond to the odor of musk, an ingredient in perfumes and colognes. (In case you don't believe that truffles are volatile, just wait for about half an hour after you have eaten some. You should be rewarded with the pleasant truffle burp.) One thing is certain—the potency of truffles is fleeting. Even after a few days, the magic trapped within begins to vanish into thin air, leaving a shadow of its former self. Unless the fresh truffle is bound with other substances (such as rice or eggs), it is gone forever. That is one of the reasons canned truffles are a culinary oxymoron. The canning process destroys all elements of the wizardry that makes truffles what they are. Use them only for decorations, please.

Should you be fortunate enough to have some fresh truffles on hand, keep them refrigerated and tightly covered. Even then, they will retain their character for only a few days. When you are ready to use them, brush the dirt off with a towel or wash them with cold running water and be ready to use them right away. Fresh truffles can be added raw to salads or shaved over pasta. I find that a little heat helps maximize their flavor, so I sauté them with whatever I am cooking. Another exciting combination with truffles is smoked meats such as sausage or smoked pheasant—the combination in cream over pasta is thrilling! Truffles like garlic and onions, also.

If you find that you have more truffles than you can use fresh, there are several ways of preserving their character. Bury the truffles in raw rice and keep the container cold. The flavor of only the very freshest truffles, however, will permeate the rice. Use about 3 or 4 cups of rice for an ounce of whole truffle. After about a week, remove the truffle and use it immediately. The rice will keep for about a month if chilled; after that the truffle flavor begins to fade. I like to preserve truffles in bourbon. The liquor takes on the truffle essence and keeps it indefinitely, and you do not need to remove the truffle later. Thinly slice one ounce of truffle and add to a fifth of good bourbon. It takes about a week for the truffle to flavor the liquor. You can also use vodka. The truffled liquor is great in a sauce needing truffle zing; just don't forget to add some of the sliced truffle to the dish.

In case you're wondering, dried truffles are worthless and frozen truffles are not much better. You will know when truffles begin to rot, because the odor becomes sickening.

Most mushroom dishes can be paired with wines, depending on the nature of the preparation. Truffles go best with Burgundy or its American version, Pinot Noir. The simultaneous explosions that occur on the palate when these two flavors meet is mind-shattering.

The Main Species of Truffles

Although truffles are not cultivated in the true sense of being reproduced artificially through control of their life cycle, they are nonetheless harvested in areas that have been carefully chosen for their reproduction—near the roots of trees with which they are associated. The French have this art down to a science, so French truffles are often referred to as cultivated. Only in the last few years has this method of cultivation been successfully reproduced in the United States, most recently by Frank Garland in North Carolina, who hopes to have a full-fledged truffle business going in the near future. What makes his truffles so special is that they are of the same species as the European black truffle, not our American truffle.

Most truffles are of the genus *Tuber,* with several related species. One domestic truffle—the Oregon black truffle—is in the genus *Picoa.*

Tuber melanosporum   Common name—black truffle, black truffle of Perigord. The most famous of all truffles, it is found by hunters who send their legendary pigs into the forest to sniff out the treasure. But dogs are actually more commonly used for two reasons: first, they are easier to train and control; and second, dogs generally do not like to eat truffles and are, therefore, much more likely to give them to a hunter. We have all seen photographs showing a truffle hunter holding one end of a long rope and a hungry pig on the other end. The black truffle is harvested with a casing or shelllike coating, which is then cut away and packaged as truffle peelings. Some black truffles have been known to grow to the size of a baseball.

Tuber magnatum   Common name—white truffle. More intense than the black truffle, the white truffle has perhaps more impassioned aficionados. It is a northern Italian specialty. A few scrapes with a specially devised grater held over pasta makes a perfect dish when paired with a glass of Gattinara.

Picoa carthusiana   Common name—Oregon black truffle. All of my recipes for truffles in this book were tested with Oregon truffles. I think they are every bit as delicious, exotic, and haunting as their European cousins. Oregon black truffles seem to grow a little larger than the white ones (see below) and have a milder flavor, mirroring the relationship between the two famous European species. Work continues on identifying other species for future consumption.

Tuber gibbosum   Common name—Oregon white truffle. Small and tan-colored, this truffle has a flavor as good as its European counterpart. Since most Italian white truffles come to this country at least several days after they have been picked, they are more mature and stronger smelling, whereas the freshly picked American version takes that extra day or two to reach the same intensity. Truffles generally develop their maximum character at full maturity and not before, and that the process continues after the truffle has been picked, owing to enzymatic activity.

Glace de Morille

The famous glace de viande *of French cuisine is a stock that is reduced until it reaches its richest and most potent concentration of flavor and intensity. The same thing can be achieved with wild mushrooms, but only using certain types. Morels and cèpes are the best candidates for this treatment, and the following is the simple method for morels.*

This is very intense stuff. The aroma is heady, the true essence of morels. This Glace de Morille will be so intense that it will taste salty without adding any salt to it. It will be thick enough to coat a spoon and have a soylike color. Use it for a sauce or a soup base. Or flavor it with a little salt and use directly on steak, lamb, or venison.

2 pounds fresh morels

Rinse the morels well. Place them in a large saucepan and cover with water. Bring to a boil over high heat and reduce heat and simmer for 45 minutes. Lift the morels out of the liquid and reserve for use in stuffing or sautéed dishes. There should be about 6 to 8 cups of liquid in the pan.

Continue to reduce the liquid until the bottom of the pan begins to darken. (This may take several hours.) Swirl around the liquid to loosen any hardened residue. Pour this liquid through a fine sieve lined with cheesecloth. Let sit for 1 hour, then pour the liquid off any settled residue.

The glaze will keep frozen for months.

Makes about $\frac{1}{3}$ cup

Fresh Morels in Caraway Sauce

Caraway and morels share the same qualities of earthy, exotic fragrance. They form a natural combination of flavors.

Although food processor manufacturers' caution you not to process potatoes, I find that processors work well if you are making a sauce.

Cut the potato into cubes, place in a small saucepan, and cover with water, adding a little salt to the water. Bring to a boil and simmer until the potato is fully cooked, about 20 minutes.

While the potato is cooking, clean the morels and slice them in half. Place the butter in a sauté pan over medium heat, and sauté the red pepper and onion. Add the morels and continue to sauté until the morels are limp and fully cooked, about 5 minutes. Season with a little salt.

1 large russet potato, peeled

4 ounces fresh morels

2 tablespoons butter

1 red bell pepper, seeded and thinly sliced

1/2 small onion, thinly sliced

Salt

3 tablespoons caraway seed

1/4 cup heavy cream

1/4 cup milk

Place the caraway seed in a small saucepan and just cover with water. Bring to a boil, then turn the heat to low and simmer for 30 minutes, adding water as necessary to keep the seed just covered. Strain the liquid into a small bowl and discard the seed.

Drain the potato and begin to process in a food processor. Add the caraway liquid, cream, and milk and puree until smooth and creamy, adding extra milk if necessary. Add salt to taste.

Divide the potato puree among 4 plates and place the morels in the center. Serve immediately.

Serves 4

Suggested wine: Stag's Leap Wine Cellar's Reserve Cabernet Sauvignon

Medallions of Lamb en Croute with Morel Duxelles and Glace de Morille

Try this variation of filet en croute for a formal dinner party. Fresh cèpes can also be used, in which case the glace should be made from fresh cèpes also.

Place oil in a large sauté pan over high heat. Heat until it just begins to smoke, then add the lamb and brown on both sides, 1 minute on each side. Remove the medallions to a plate lined with a paper towel to drain excess fat. Let cool on the plate.

In another sauté pan, heat the butter over medium heat and sauté the morels, green pepper, and onion 2 to 3 minutes, or until the liquid is mostly evaporated. Season with the salt, sugar, and soy sauce and let the duxelles cool.

Roll out each square of puff pastry dough to about double its original size. Cut each rolled-out dough square into 4 equal pieces. Refrigerate for 15 minutes.

¼ cup vegetable oil

8 medallions of lamb, 2 to 3 ounces each, cut from the rack or loin, trimmed of all fat and sinew

2 tablespoons butter

4 ounces fresh morels, finely chopped

⅓ cup finely chopped green bell pepper

⅓ cup finely chopped onion

¼ teaspoon salt

¼ teaspoon sugar

½ teaspoon soy sauce

2 5-inch squares all-butter puff pastry (available frozen in grocery stores)

1 egg, lightly beaten

⅓ cup Glace de Morille (page 60)

Preheat the oven to 450° F.

Lay one piece of puff pastry on a table or cutting board. Place some of the duxelles on top of a medallion of lamb, then place so the duxelles side is against the puff pastry. Fold the corners of the puff pastry over the lamb to enclose it completely. Turn the pastry-covered lamb over and brush a little beaten egg over the top. Cut a decorative pattern into the puff pastry. Repeat for the remaining lamb.

Place the pastry packages on a baking sheet lined with foil and bake for about 15 minutes. Place 2 teaspoons of Glace de Morille on each of 4 plates. Place 2 pastry packages on each plate and serve immediately. The lamb should be medium-rare.

Serves 4

Suggested wine: Older Heitz Cabernet Sauvignon, Bella Oaks Vineyard

Morel Sauce

As much as I love to pick and eat fresh morels, when I use them to make a sauce it always comes out somewhat cloudy. Morels should really be dried for making a clean, clear sauce. What's more, you can make this sauce at any time of the year because you can hunt for dried morels at your favorite specialty food store when they are out of season. This sauce is ideal for veal, chicken, or game birds.

---

1 teaspoon caraway seed

3 tablespoons chopped onion

*3 tablespoons chopped
green bell pepper*

2 tablespoons clarified butter

1 teaspoon sugar

1 teaspoon salt

1 tablespoon soy sauce

1 ounce dried morels

*1 tablespoon arrowroot mixed
with 1 tablespoon cold water*

Place the caraway seed, onion, green pepper, butter, sugar, salt, and soy sauce in a small saucepan. Add 3 cups of water and bring to a boil, then simmer over medium heat for 30 minutes. Strain through a fine sieve or cheesecloth and return liquid to saucepan. Add the morels and simmer for another 30 minutes.

Stir in the arrowroot mixture if sauce is to be used immediately, and stir over low heat until thickened.

Note: If you want to store this sauce for future use, freeze without thickening with arrowroot. Reheat and thicken before serving.

Makes 2 cups

Morels Rosenthal in Kataifi Nests

I named this dish for the late Jack Rosenthal, who was a founder of the Culinary Institute of America and later came to Philadelphia's Monell Institute to work on sensory evaluation of food and wine. This is still my favorite preparation for morels and is always the way we make the first morels of the season. The kataifi—shredded phyllo—can be easily found in Italian or Greek grocery stores, usually sitting right next to the phyllo pastry. In Greece and Turkey, kataifi is mainly used for sweet pastries. Kataifi nests are a very good way to serve any braised mushroom dishes as a first course. They can also be used to surround ragouts used for main courses.

Preheat the oven to 300° F.

Heat 2 tablespoons of the butter in a large sauté pan. Add the onion and bell pepper and sauté over medium heat for 1 minute. Add the morels, lower the heat, and cover the pan with a lid. Over a low heat, allow the morels to cook and give off their liquid for about 30 minutes.

While the morels are braising, make a roux: combine 2 tablespoons of the butter with the flour and stir over medium heat in a small sauté pan. Stir until the roux becomes golden brown. Set aside.

Also while the morels are braising, form each kataifi strand into a circle and place on a lined baking sheet. Melt the remaining 2 tablespoons butter and drizzle over the kataifi, then sprinkle the fresh herbs on top. Place the kataifi in the oven and bake until light golden and crispy, 10 to 15 minutes. Set aside until ready to use. (This step can be done well in advance. The nests will hold for several days, covered, in a cool location.)

Add the salt, sugar, and soy sauce to the morels and stir well. Bring the liquid to a low simmer and, while stirring, gradually add the roux. Different morels can yield different amounts of liquid, so the thickening process must be done carefully; you may not have to use all the roux. Stir until thickened. If the roux is insufficient, you can make a little more, but be very careful not to overthicken. This mixture tends to become more thick as it stands.

Place a single kataifi nest on a serving plate, fill each one with morels, and serve.

Serves 4
Suggested wine: Freemark Abbey Cabernet Sauvignon

---

6 tablespoons butter
⅓ cup chopped onion
⅓ cup chopped green bell pepper
1 pound fresh morels, sliced
2 tablespoons flour
2 ounces kataifi, divided into 4 long individual pieces
½ cup fresh herbs, such as savory, thyme, oregano, or basil, chopped
1 teaspoon salt
1 teaspoon sugar
1 tablespoon soy sauce

Morel Enchiladas

The key to making a good enchilada is to create a filling that is distinctive enough so that its taste will come through the tortilla and the melted cheese topping. You may be surprised to learn that morels are regularly found in Mexico and excellent-quality Mexican morels are imported into this country in fairly large quantities.

This dish makes a good alternative vegetarian item for a Mexican buffet. I like to serve it with a salad of sliced asparagus, chopped papaya, scallions, and cilantro tossed with a little oil and vinegar and seasoned with a little salt.

If poblano chiles are not available, use Anaheim or New Mexico chiles. As a last resort, use bell peppers but add a diced chile, such as serrano or jalapeño.

> *6 tablespoons butter*
> *1 large onion, thinly sliced*
> *2 poblano chiles, seeded, stemmed, and thinly sliced*
> *1 pound fresh morels, sliced lengthwise in half or 2 ounces dried, reconstituted in 2 cups water and sliced (reserve liquid)*
> *Vegetable oil*
> *8 corn tortillas*
> *1 teaspoon salt*
> *1 teaspoon sugar*
> *1 tablespoon soy sauce*
> *2 tablespoons flour*
> *2 cups grated Monterey Jack cheese (8 ounces)*

Melt 4 tablespoons of the butter in a skillet. Add the onion and chiles and sauté for 2 to 3 minutes over medium heat, until they begin to wilt. Add the fresh morels, turn the heat to low, and cover the skillet with a lid. This will draw liquid from the mushrooms, which is an important part of this process. Simmer for 10 minutes. (If you are using dried morels, add the morels now also and sauté for 1 minute, then add the reserved liquid, cover, and proceed to the next step.)

Meanwhile, heat a little oil in another skillet. One by one, place a tortilla in the skillet and heat for 30 seconds on each side. The tortillas will lose their brittleness and become pliable enough to fold. As each tortilla is done, place it on a paper towel and continue until all the tortillas are softened. Keep warm on the counter until ready to assemble the dish.

Preheat the oven to 425° F.

Add the salt, sugar, and soy sauce to the morels and simmer for another 5 minutes, if necessary adding a little water to keep mixture immersed. Strain through a fine sieve, squeezing the morels as much as possible. Reserve the liquid; there should be ¾ to 1 cup.

Evenly divide the mushroom mixture among the tortillas. Roll the mixture up in the tortillas and arrange side by side in a glass baking dish.

Add the remaining 2 tablespoons butter to the skillet and set over low heat. Add the flour and blend thoroughly to make a roux. Stir over medium heat until the roux begins to lightly brown, in about 4 minutes. Immediately add the reserved liquid and stir until the sauce is thickened. (Adjust thickening if necessary by adding a little water or further reducing.)

Spread the sauce on the enchiladas, then sprinkle the cheese evenly over the top. Cover the dish with aluminum foil and place in the middle of the oven. Bake for 20 to 30 minutes, or until all the cheese is melted and the enchiladas are hot inside. Remove from the oven, let stand for 10 minutes, then remove the foil and serve.

Serves 4
Suggested wine: Sutter Home Zinfandel

Green Beans with Truffles and Oyster Sauce

This is usually served as a side dish. However, as a first course, I place the beans over thin rice noodles that have been seasoned with a little sauce and sesame oil.

You must use fresh truffles for this dish, either American or European.

---

8 ounces green beans, cut into 2-inch lengths

2 tablespoons vegetable oil

1½ ounces fresh truffles, thinly sliced

1 (2-ounce) can water chestnuts, drained and thinly sliced

2 teaspoons Chinese oyster sauce

---

for 3 minutes. Remove beans from water and drain. Set aside.

Heat the oil in a skillet. Add the beans, truffles, and water chestnuts and stir over a medium heat for about 2 minutes. Stir in the oyster sauce until it uniformly coats the beans, then serve.

Bring about 4 quarts of lightly salted water to a boil in a saucepan. Add the green beans and cook

Serves 4
Suggested accompaniment: Sparkling water

Rings, Diamonds, and Corn

Eric Miller is a roguish figure right out of the swashbuckling pages of Sabatini. He roams the countryside, wine glass in hand, preaching the good life. At home is his witty, intelligent wife, Lee, keeping hearth and business books in order. Together they make one of the most potent business teams in the United States. Heidi and I have been privileged to know them almost since the beginning of their Chaddsford Winery in Chadds Ford, Pennsylvania. A few years ago, we served a wine dinner for Lee and Eric, showcasing their new releases. Among the dishes was to be a new one that would pair with Eric's new Chardonnay. In fact, the name came before the conception of the dish.

Make the panade. Scald the milk in a medium saucepan. Add the butter and stir until melted. Then sift in the flour and stir vigorously over medium heat for 5 minutes, taking care not to burn the mixture. Remove from heat and let cool for 10 minutes. Blend in 1 of the egg yolks and set aside.

THE PANADE
¾ *cup milk*
2 tablespoons butter
¾ *cup all-purpose flour*
3 egg yolks

THE MOUSSE
6 ears fresh corn
½ *red or green bell pepper, cored, seeded, and sliced*
1 tablespoon curry powder
1 teaspoon salt
4 eggs

THE RED PEPPER PUREE
2 large red bell peppers
3 tablespoons fresh lemon juice
1 tablespoon sugar
½ *teaspoon salt*

THE MORELS
½ *ounce dried morels*
1 teaspoon soy sauce
Salt
1 tablespoon vegetable oil

Preheat the oven to 325° F.

Remove the corn kernels from the ears with a sharp knife. You should have about 1½ cups. Pick out the nicest kernels and set aside, leaving 1 cup kernels for the mousse.

Place the 1 cup kernels, the bell pepper, curry powder, and salt in a saucepan. Add enough water to cover. Bring to a boil and simmer for 10 minutes. Remove from heat and drain.

In a blender or food processor, combine the drained corn mixture with ⅓ cup of the panade (use the rest in another recipe or discard), whole eggs, and remaining 2 egg yolks and process until smooth. Strain through a fine sieve.

Bring a large kettle of water to a boil.

Line the bottom of a well-buttered 2-quart pâté or loaf pan with waxed paper. Pour in the mousse mixture. Place in a larger baking dish and pour in boiling water to come halfway up pan.

(continued on page 70)

Rings, Diamonds, and Corn

(*continued from page 69*)

Cover pâté or loaf pan with aluminum foil and place in oven. Bake for 30 minutes. Remove pâté pan from the water bath and chill, uncovered, in refrigerator until set, about 2 hours.

Preheat the broiler. Place the peppers in a pan and put in broiler. Broil for 10 to 12 minutes, or until the skins shrivel and begin to blacken. Place in a paper bag and let cool. Peel the skin entirely from the peppers, then slit them open and remove the stem, seeds, and veins.

Place the roasted peppers in a blender or food processor and add the lemon juice, sugar, and salt. Blend to a smooth puree. Set aside. Turn oven down to 200° F.

Place the morels in a small saucepan and cover with water. Add the soy sauce and some salt, then bring to a boil and simmer for 20 minutes. Remove from heat, drain, and let cool. Cut the morels crosswise to make thin rings. Reserve the tip and stems for another use. Combine the morel rings with the reserved corn kernels.

Place the vegetable oil in a skillet and sauté the morel rings with the corn kernels, lightly salting for taste, until the kernels are tender, about 2 minutes. Set aside and keep warm.

Run a knife along the sides of the mousse and turn out onto a flat plate. Cut into 6 even pieces, then place in the warm oven.

In a blender or food processor, combine the watercress, 2 tablespoons water, and the vinegar until pureed. Pour into a medium saucepan and add the cream. Bring to a simmer and add fish sauce to taste. If necessary, thicken lightly by adding the cornstarch mixture and cooking until slightly thickened. Keep warm.

Put the red pepper puree in a medium saucepan and warm gently. Keep warm.

Place about 1 tablespoon of the red pepper puree in the centers of 6 individual serving plates. Place a slice of corn mousse on top, then put the morel-corn mixture on top of the mousse. Pour the watercress sauce around the edge of the red pepper puree. With a toothpick, start in the watercress sauce and draw a line into the red pepper puree. Repeat around each plate to give a "scalloped" appearance. Garnish the top with dill or fennel. Serve immediately.

Serves 6

Suggested wine: Chaddsford Winery Chardonnay

THE WATERCRESS SAUCE

½ ounce fresh watercress, stems removed

1½ teaspoons vinegar

¾ cup heavy cream

Vietnamese fish sauce (available in Asian markets) to taste

1 tablespoon cornstarch blended with 1 tablespoon cold water (optional)

Sprigs of fresh dill or fennel, for garnish

Morels with Ruffled Pasta

Among the many varieties of pasta, the best with morels is the ruffled kind or, better yet, a "ruffle trio" of plain pasta, spinach pasta, and tomato pasta. The tight consistency blends well with the texture of the morels.

Bring about 6 quarts of lightly salted water to a boil and add the pasta. Stir and cook for about 10 minutes, until the pasta reaches the consistency that you like.

Place the dried morels in a small saucepan and cover with 2 cups water. Bring to a boil and simmer for 20 minutes. You should have about 1 cup of liquid. Remove the morels from the liquid and cut them to approximate the size of the pasta. Return to the liquid.

---

6 ounces ruffled pasta (radiatore)

½ ounce dried morels, or 6 ounces fresh, cleaned and cut to approximate size of cooked pasta

2 tablespoons vegetable oil or melted butter

1 small onion, thinly sliced

1 small red or green bell pepper, thinly sliced

1 teaspoon salt

1 teaspoon sugar

1 tablespoon soy sauce

1 tablespoon arrowroot mixed with 1 tablespoon cold water

While the pasta is cooking and the mushrooms are simmering, heat the oil or butter in a skillet. Add the onion and bell pepper and sauté for 1 minute over high heat. Add the morels. (If you are using fresh morels, lower the heat so that the liquid can be drawn from the mushrooms.) Stir in the salt, sugar, and soy sauce. Simmer for another minute, then add the arrowroot mixture and cook gently until the sauce thickens, about 1 minute more.

Drain the pasta, transfer to a bowl, and toss with the morels. Serve immediately.

Serves 4

Suggested wine: Neyers Napa Valley Cabernet Sauvignon

Scallops with Asparagus, Chèvre, and Morels

Morels and asparagus are twin harbingers of that culinary paradise called spring. Winter loosens its icy grip and melts into the ground, which erupts with nature's green. This is a celebration dish.

Preheat the oven to very low, 175° to 200° F.

Scald the cream in a small saucepan. Add the dill, cognac, salt, and stock, stirring over medium heat until sauce begins to thicken. Remove from the heat, cover, and keep warm.

Place the chèvre on a baking dish lined with foil and warm in oven, about 2 to 3 minutes.

Put the oil and garlic in a sauté pan and sauté over medium heat for 30 seconds. Add the asparagus and red pepper, and sauté for another minute or until asparagus is tender.

1 cup heavy cream

½ teaspoon dried dill

1 teaspoon cognac

¼ teaspoon salt

¼ cup rich lobster or shrimp stock or clam juice

4 slices chèvre, such as Montrachet, in ¾-inch pieces

2 tablespoons vegetable oil

2 garlic cloves, finely chopped

¼ pound thin asparagus, trimmed to within 4 inches from top

1 tablespoon finely diced red bell pepper

8 medium fresh morels, sliced in half lengthwise, or 16 whole small morels (or any other fresh mushroom)

¼ pound fresh scallops, cut into thin (¼-inch) slices

¼ pound medium shrimp, peeled and deveined

Salt

(This may take longer if the asparagus is not pencil-thin.) Add the morels and sauté for an additional minute. The morels will give off liquid. Continue to sauté until the moisture is gone. Add the scallops and shrimp, increase the heat to high, and stir-fry until the scallops are milky white and the shrimps curl, about 2 to 3 minutes. Lightly salt to taste.

Divide the warmed sauce evenly among 4 warmed serving dishes. In the center of each plate place a slice of chèvre. Divide the scallop mixture among the 4 plates, leaning the tips of the asparagus over the chèvre. Serve immediately.

Serves 4

Suggested wine: Sanford Sauvignon Blanc

Stuffed Morels Marie

When I first made this dish I wanted to dedicate it to my wife, Heidi. But she modestly opposed naming it after herself. Her full first name, however, is Heidemarie, so we compromised, and along with the alliteration, we think it worked out well.

The recipe can be made with fresh morels, but you must first sweat them. Place about ½ pound of morels in a large saucepan. Add about ½ inch of water, bring the liquid to a boil, then cover and turn down to a simmer. Let cook for 30 minutes. The liquid should be covering the mushrooms by this time; if not, add a little more water. Unlike the liquid from dried morels, this liquid will be gray and somewhat cloudy, which is fine for this cream sauce but not for a clear sauce. Use the liquid as you would the liquid from dried morels, remembering to flavor it accordingly.

THE MOUSSE STUFFING
⅓ cup chopped raw pheasant or chicken, cleaned and free of sinew
1 tablespoon panade (see page 69)
½ teaspoon onion powder
½ teaspoon garlic powder
1 teaspoon white wine vinegar
½ teaspoon dried thyme
1 egg
¼ cup heavy cream
Salt and pepper

THE MUSHROOMS AND SAUCE
1 large green bell pepper
⅓ cup chopped onion
1 teaspoon caraway seed
1 teaspoon salt
1 teaspoon sugar
1 teaspoon soy sauce
16 medium to large dried morel caps (about 1 to 1½ ounces)
½ cup heavy cream
1 tablespoon arrowroot mixed with 1 tablespoon cold water
12 chives, cut into 3-inch strips

In a food processor, blend the pheasant, panade, onion powder, garlic powder, vinegar, thyme, egg, and cream until smooth. The mixture should be fairly thick, like cake icing, so it can be piped through a very small fitting for a pastry bag. Correct consistency by adding either more cream or more meat to make thinner or thicker, respectively. Now test the mousse by placing a little in a skillet and sautéing it over medium heat for a couple of minutes. This will cook the mousse quickly and give you an idea of what it will be like when cooked inside the morels. Adjust seasonings accordingly.

Spoon the mousse into a pastry bag fitted with a tip that will fit into the bottom opening of the narrowest morel. Place bag on a plate and refrigerate.

Put 2 cups of water in a 2-quart saucepan and

bring to a simmer. Cut 4 crosswise thin rings from the center of the green pepper and set aside. Chop the rest of the pepper coarsely and place in the water. Add the onion, caraway seed, salt, sugar, and soy sauce and simmer for 30 minutes. Strain the liquid and place back in the saucepan.

Add the morels to the saucepan and simmer for another 30 minutes. Strain, leaving the liquid in the saucepan; you should have about 1 cup. Snip off and discard the stems of the morels right up and slightly into the base. (This is necessary to ensure the opening is big enough for the pastry tip to enter.) Let cool.

Remove the mousse-filled pastry bag from the refrigerator and pipe the mousse into the base of each morel. The mousse should be thick enough so that it does not run back out of the morels after stuffing.

Pour $\frac{1}{3}$ cup of the morel liquid into a small saucepan. Bring the remaining $\frac{2}{3}$ cup morel liquid to a simmer and add the cream. Adjust for salt and add some of the arrowroot mixture, stirring until thickened. Bring the morel liquid in the saucepan to a light boil and thicken with the remaining arrowroot mixture. Keep both sauces warm.

Fill the bottom of a steamer with about 2 inches of water. Bring the water to a boil, and then reduce heat to a simmer. Place the stuffed morels and pepper rings on a plate that will fit into the steamer. Steam for 20 minutes. The mousse should be firm.

Place a pepper ring in the center of each dinner plate. Place the morels, standing up and leaning against each other, inside the pepper ring. Pour a little of the clear sauce directly over the morels. Then surround the outside of the ring with the morel cream sauce. Finally place 3 chives flared out from the pepper ring to the edge of each plate and serve immediately.

Serves 4
Suggested wine: Cabernet Sauvignon, preferably Heitz

Truffle Tart with Stilton and Stinging Nettles

You can use white or black, French or Italian truffles for this. Also, any aged blue cheeses, such as Roquefort or Gorgonzola, can be used instead of Stilton, and spinach can be substituted for the nettles. If you use fresh nettles, be sure to handle them with gloves until they have been cooked.

Preheat the oven to 450° F.

Sauté the onion, garlic, truffles, and nettles or spinach in the butter for 1 minute over medium heat, then cover and cook over low heat for 5 minutes. Remove lid and stir. If greens are not completely wilted, cover and cook until they are. Salt very lightly.

Meanwhile, beat the milk, cream, eggs, and, if using canned truffles, 1 tablespoon truffle liquid.

---

1 small onion, finely diced

1 garlic clove, minced

1 tablespoon thinly sliced fresh truffles (canned may be used, but use the juice in the custard preparation)

2 cups fresh stinging nettles or spinach

2 tablespoons butter

Salt

½ cup milk

½ cup heavy cream

2 eggs

1 prebaked 9-inch pie crust

5 ounces Stilton cheese, crumbled

Place the truffle mixture on the bottom of the pie crust, spreading it evenly. Then sprinkle the Stilton over the mixture. Cover with the milk mixture, submerging all the cheese under the liquid.

Bake the tart for 10 minutes, then reduce oven to 350° F. and bake for 20 minutes more. Check for doneness by piercing with a fork, which should come out clean. Let rest for 15 minutes before serving. This tart can be cooled to room temperature, refrigerated, then reheated for 7 minutes in a 325° F. oven before serving.

Serves 6

Suggested wine: rich, heady Pinot Noir, preferably from David Bruce or Santa Cruz Mountain Vineyard

Spoon Bread with Morel Stems

Our family began vacationing in Cape May, New Jersey, about fifteen years ago. We come back each year because of a Victorian-era hotel called the Chalfonte. Breakfast is notable for its spoon bread, a Southern specialty, which is served with warm biscuits, coffee, bacon, and eggs.

Pairing this rich soufflelike preparation with mushrooms is tricky. Morel stems are ideal because they are firmer than the caps. (Stems of other mushrooms can also be used, such as domestic button mushrooms or portobellos, but not shiitake stems, which are always tough.) The flavor of the cornmeal is quite rich, so you must be sure to season the mushroom mixture well before adding it to the batter.

1 tablespoon butter

2 to 3 ounces morel stems, finely diced

½ small green bell pepper, finely diced

½ small onion, finely diced

Salt

2½ cups milk

1 cup yellow cornmeal

5 eggs, separated

Melt the butter in a sauté pan over medium heat and add the mushroom stems, bell pepper, and onion. Sauté for 2 to 3 minutes, until the mushroom stems are tender. (You can also turn the heat down and cover the mixture and let cook for about 10 minutes. Just be sure that there is enough liquid in the pan so it does not burn, since stems are generally much drier than caps and will not give off as much liquid during braising.) Season with salt until the flavor is very well defined, then salt just a bit more. Set aside.

Scald the milk in a 2-quart saucepan. Add 1½ teaspoons salt and then the cornmeal, stirring continuously over a low heat. You will need to stir more vigorously as you add the last of the cornmeal because the mixture will begin to thicken. Stir well so the cornmeal is as smooth as possible. Let cool to room temperature.

Preheat the oven to 400° F.

Beat the egg whites until stiff. Stir the egg yolks and mushrooms into the cornmeal and blend well. Fold in the egg whites.

Spoon the mixture into either several small ramekins or a 2-quart soufflé dish. Bake the ramekins for 5 minutes or until browned on top; bake the larger dish for 6 to 9 minutes. Lower the heat to 325° F. and continue baking until the spoon bread is set, 10 to 15 minutes for ramekins and 35 minutes for large dish. The inside should not be runny, but neither should it be too dry. Serve hot.

Serves 4 to 6

Rigatoni with Truffles and Kielbasa

Truffles pair wonderfully with cured or smoked meats. A simple example follows, but prosciutto or smoked duck works just as well as kielbasa.

Bring a large pot of lightly salted water to a boil. Add the rigatoni and cook until the rigatoni is al dente, about 10 minutes. Drain.

While the pasta is cooking place the oil in a skillet over medium heat. Add the onion and garlic and sauté for about 1 minute. Add the truffles and kielbasa and sauté for another 2 minutes.

6 ounces rigatoni or other large, tubular pasta
4 tablespoons vegetable oil
½ small onion, diced
4 garlic cloves, finely diced
1 ounce fresh truffles, thinly sliced
4 ounces kielbasa (Polish sausage), cut into matchstick pieces
Salt

Season with salt to taste, then toss with the rigatoni and serve.

Variation: As the dish is completed, add ¾ cup of heavy cream to the truffle mixture and heat until the cream thickens. Keep on low heat and continue to heat for another 5 minutes, adding some milk if the mixture gets too thick. (This allows the truffle essence to permeate the cream sauce.) This sauce is also good reheated.

Serves 4

Suggested wine: Pinot Noir

Lobster Lasagna with Chèvre and Morels

My finest recollection of lobster feasting is an experience Heidi and I had several years ago when visiting our friends Mike and M. L. Rilley, in Winter Harbor, Maine. There one doesn't simply crack open a fresh lobster with the instruments at the table. Even in Maine lobster is for special occasions. It should consumed on a rocky beach, the shells cracked open with a handy rock. The lobster will have been steamed in a large pot with sea water, set over an open fire built on the beach. This is lobster eating at its most basic and so it was on that memorable trip.

Yet lobster also lends itself to stylized treatment in a restaurant or at home. If you prefer to eat lobster with less fuss and mess, try the following recipe, which accentuates the rich sweet taste of the lobster, contrasted with the sharp flavor of chèvre and the crunch of morels.

The lobster and subsequent stock can be made well in advance. In fact, I recommend doing it the day before. The lobster meat can be kept refrigerated for 2 days. The same is true for the morels and chèvre. The pasta may be made ahead, dried, and kept indefinitely. If used dried, adjust the cooking time accordingly.

Blend the chèvre and cream cheese thoroughly in a bowl with the dill. Refrigerate overnight. Remove from refrigerator about 1 hour before you intend to use it in the recipe.

Place about 3 inches of water in a large pot. Bring to a boil and add the salt. Carefully add the lobsters. Cover the pot with a tight-fitting lid and let the lobsters steam for 20 minutes. Remove lobsters from the water with tongs and let cool. Bring the steaming water to a low simmer, skimming off any scum.

Carefully remove the meat from the lobsters by cracking the shells and coaxing out the meat, keeping it as intact as possible. Be especially careful when removing the meat from the claws and tails. Cut the tail meat into $1/2$-inch-wide medallions and reserve.

THE CHÈVRE
2 ounces chèvre,
at room temperature

2 ounces cream cheese,
at room temperature

$1/2$ teaspoon dried dill

THE LOBSTER
1 tablespoon salt

4 small live lobsters,
1–$1\,1/4$ pounds each

THE MORELS
$1/4$ teaspoon salt

$1/2$ teaspoon caraway seed

$1/4$ cup chopped green bell pepper

$1/2$ ounce dried morels

THE PASTA
Several long sheets thin fresh
pasta (about $1/2$ pound)

Pizelle maker (optional)

THE SAUCE
$1/2$ cup heavy cream

$1/2$ cup milk

1 tablespoon cognac

2 teaspoons tomato paste

1 tablespoon cornstarch mixed
with 1 tablespoon cold water
(optional)

Salt

Dill sprigs, for garnish

With a hammer, break up the rest of the shells and break off the small legs. The smaller you can break the pieces of the shell, the better. Place the shells in the simmering water and add enough water to barely cover the shells. Bring to a boil and cover tightly with a lid. Reduce to a simmer and boil for 1 hour. Remove the lid, and let stock reduce to about $1/2$ inch. Strain and measure the stock; you should have about $1/2$ cup of rich stock. Cool and set aside.

For the morels, combine the salt, caraway seed, green pepper, and 1 cup water in a small saucepan and bring to a boil. Let simmer and reduce for 30 minutes. Strain the liquid and return to the saucepan. Add the morels, bring back to a boil, reduce heat, and simmer for 20 minutes. Lift the morels out of the liquid and set aside. Bring stock to a boil and reduce to about 2 tablespoons. Add this liquid to the lobster stock.

From the sheets of pasta, cut 12 rounds of dough using a 4-inch round cookie cutter. If desired, press these rounds in a pizelle iron to yield a decorative pattern. Keep covered.

Preheat the oven to 250° F.

Bring a large pot of lightly salted water to a boil and add the pasta. Cook the pasta until al dente and drain.

While the pasta is cooking, make the sauce and the lobster mixture. In a medium saucepan, combine the cream, milk, cognac, and tomato paste. Simmer over low heat until the tomato paste is well incorporated, then add the lobster stock and morel liquid and simmer for 5 minutes more. You should have about $1 1/2$ cups of sauce. Stir in some of the cornstarch mixture and heat until lightly thickened. The sauce should be only thick enough to coat a spoon. Add the morels and lobster meat, and simmer gently for another 2 minutes. You may have to adjust for thickness again so the mixture is not runny. Remove from the heat, season with salt if necessary, and keep warm.

Lay out 4 pieces of pasta on a lined baking sheet and spread the chèvre mixture among them. Place in the warm oven to soften the cheese, about 10 minutes.

Put the cheese-topped pasta rounds on 4 dinner plates. Cover each with another pasta round, then spoon the lobster sauce on top. Place a final pasta layer on top of each plate and garnish with dill sprigs. Serve immediately.

Serves 4
Suggested wine: Chalone Chardonnay or Roederer Estate Champagne

Cèpe

THE KING AND LESSER NOBILITY

Cèpes and Their Cousins

On the top of the refrigerator in my parents' kitchen is a very small jar. Inside are two shrunken mushrooms and a yellowed piece of paper that reads "*Boletus edulis*—found by Jackie [that's me] in State Game Lands, 8/25/66." I know it's still there because my mother knew just where to look when I called her to ask about it. After my father read me what it said, he did what I knew he would. He opened the jar, sniffed it, and said, "They smell just as good as they did twenty-eight years ago." Whenever people in my family see that jar they all do the same thing—open, sniff, and sigh. The rich, sweet woodiness is still there and may still be there until the end of time, for it is the scent of a real *Boletus edulis,* hinting of the pleasures buried deep in the forest, and rare as gold. Rare in our neck of the woods, anyway, which has few spots where this most revered of mushrooms can be found. We don't find many around here, and even though we have discovered some since 1966, and have dried them, they do not compare to those two little jewels sitting atop that refrigerator at Mom and Pop's.

I remember the first time I ordered dried cèpes from the West Coast, back in the 1970s. Inside the bag were beautiful, perfectly cut slices of what were called porcini. I stuck my head in as far as it would go, and took a deep breath. Nothing. I inhaled again, harder. I sensed a papery, vague, dried mushroom smell, but the bells did not go off. What a disappointment. Since then I've reconciled myself to the fact that there are few true cèpes sold in this country. The field guides declare emphatically that cèpes are plentiful in the West, and indeed the fresh specimens I have seen certainly look like cèpes and are wonderful when cooked fresh, but it is only when they are dried that the real test comes, and none that I have seen have passed. Only from Europe have I received what I consider to be the real *Boletus edulis,* where I could dive into the bag, inhale, and emerge with a smile that comes only from air enriched by true cèpe essence.

Boletus edulis is truly the king among mushrooms. When asked to name a favorite I always demur, but when pressed I always choose these as the best of all. Yet it is a mushroom that reveals its magical glory only when dried, and the elements and character of the mushroom become distilled into an elixir. What is left was best described by Alexander Dumas, who declared on drinking Le Montrachet that it could be taken only "on bended knee with bowed head." Fresh cèpes are also great. There is no better grilling mushroom. It's just that when I walk through our dining room at Joe's and someone has ordered Mushrooms Krakow Style (page 88) enriched with cèpe essence, it still sends my senses soaring. The aroma fills the dining room. Only truffles compete for sensory satisfaction.

The *Boletus edulis* is one of a larger group of mushrooms known collectively as boletes. The boletes differ from the other major group, the agarics, in that they have dense pores on the underside of the cap instead of gills, which are the defining trait of agarics. Most other mushrooms described in this book are agarics, and they all have the characteristic gill structure on the underside. Boletes as a group also tend to be somewhat meatier than agarics because their caps consist of these pores as well as the fleshy cap. This double layer gives more substance to the mushrooms but also has its drawbacks. When the mushrooms become wet, the porous underside can get waterlogged and then must be cut away and discarded. In older specimens the pores usually need to be cut away anyway because they become mushy. Also, insects like to settle in between the pores and cap flesh, and you won't always see their tracks from inspecting the pores alone. Happily, there are species in this group with pores that are very tight and as firm as the cap itself. Among these varieties is the *Boletus edulis,* or king bolete. Even large mature caps are very firm and succulent. But there are other, much lesser known varieties that share this trait and are almost equal in quality.

When selecting fresh boletes, test the stem for firmness. If the stem gives or feels hollow, then it is infested with insects. All *Boletus* stems should be firm; they are excellent to eat. Also feel the underside of the cap—the pores should be dry and firm. This should be no problem if the specimens are young, but you may find a problem with older ones. All boletes should be thoroughly cooked, because they have a reputation for causing upset stomachs when eaten raw. Realize, however, that fresh clean caps will still absorb moisture during cooking and many varieties tend to get mushy when cooked. You can eliminate this problem by removing the pores before cooking. You can usually tell which caps will be a problem by pressing your fingers into the pores. If you can press easily, or if pressing leaves an indentation (not a color change; that is different), the underside will become mushy. Sautéing over medium-high heat is a good way to cook boletes, but remember that the pores tend to soak up cooking oils and liquids so you'll have to replenish the pan when necessary. Large caps are wonderful grilled, best if first brushed with some butter or oil, but make sure that the cap is fully cooked, not just heated on the outside. Sprinkling on Parmesan cheese just before the cap is done is also a favorite method of flavoring. If you are going to preserve boletes, canning is all right, but you should remove the pores unless they are very firm. I do not recommend pickling boletes; the vinegar tends to rob them of their rich flavor, which does not go well with acids.

Dried boletes come two ways: dried cèpes or porcini (same thing) and everything else. The cèpe has become so dominant and recognizable that, except in countries where everybody picks wild mushrooms, all other boletes are tossed together and sold with names like forest mushrooms or even Polish mushrooms. (This is a shame because the Polish *Boletus edulis* is the finest in the world, and the only mushroom that is available dried whole.)

When buying mushrooms labeled "cèpes" or "porcini," let your nose lead you. The mushrooms should have a rich, woodsy character with overtones of leather. Often, mature specimens lose their intensity; also, the larger, better-looking sliced mushrooms will not have the richness of smaller dried cèpes. If you buy boletes other than cèpes and porcini, you will notice a more musty woodsy character, which cèpes should never have. Some other varieties even have a slightly acrid odor, which is characteristic of the closely related genus *Suillus.* These are by far the least expensive mushrooms in this family and are still very good for cooking. When buying any dried boletes, check the mushrooms for holes. Sometimes the best mushrooms are canned while the wormy ones are dried. They're still all right for cooking unless you find this too unappetizing. Also, many cèpes have sand that must be removed before using. Cover the mushrooms with water and soak over-night, then rinse thoroughly. Strain the soaking liquid into another saucepan and return the mush-rooms to the strained liquid and proceed with the recipe.

Dried cèpes are very easy to use. Just pop them into a long-cooking stew and let them cast their magic. Or cover the mushrooms with water, bring to boil, simmer them, and watch the liquid be-come black with richness. Use that liquid as the base of a soup or sauce. This will make the liquid much more flavorful. Remember, the magic is in the liquid, not the reconstituted mushroom.

Varieties of Boletes

All of the following mushrooms are wild. No boletes have yet been successfully cultivated.

Boletus edulis   Common name—king bolete, cèpe, *Steinpilz,* porcini, *cep, borovicki.* The king of wild mushrooms, the *Boletus edulis,* is widely picked in Europe, both East and West. It is sold in every country where it is picked. The mushrooms are generally graded according to size and on the extent of insect infestation. They are most often sold dried, but are also available canned (from Germany and Switzerland) or frozen (Spain). China is emerging as an exporter of cèpes as well. The mushrooms are also found in Mexico, where some Italian companies have purchased land rights to pick them.

The *Boletus* Group   This consists of mushrooms other than the cèpe but within the genus *Boletus.* Those most commonly picked and enjoyed by wild mushroom hunters are *B. bicolor* (red and yel-low bolete), *B. mirabilis, B. appendiculatus* (butter bolete), *B. barrowsii* (white king bolete), *B. aureus, B. affinis.* All of these mushrooms are excellent and we especially enjoy *B. appendiculatus,* which is very firm and particularly tasty. My father prefers it to *B. edulis!* In the western United States, mushroom hunters enjoy *B. aureus* and *B. barrowsii,* and claim they are the equal of *B. edulis.* By any measure, this is the varsity squad of wild mushrooms and a hunter considers himself lucky to find any of these in quantity.

The *Tylopilus* Group Nearly identical to members of the genus *Boletus,* these mushrooms are also great finds. They include the dazzling *T. alboater,* which looks like a bolete that has been upholstered with black velour. Also good are *T. chromapes* and *T. indecisus.*

The *Leccinum* Group Another bolete group, these are distinguished by their firm, meaty character. The most famous is *L. auruntiacum* (beech bolete).

The *Strobilomyces* Group This genus contains our wise old friend, *S. strobilaceus* (old-man-of-the-woods), the name of which drips trippingly off the tongue. It grows from June through September in eastern Pennsylvania, often when nothing else is up.

The *Suillus* Group Fundamentally different from the rest of the boletes, these mushrooms are nonetheless widely picked and appreciated throughout the world. They do not have the long stems of the other boletes and are generally not as meaty, but they make up for it by growing (usually) in significant numbers. The most prolific are the famous *S. luteus* (slippery jack), which must be peeled before eating; *S. granulatus,* found on golf courses near white pine along with *S. americanus,* which turns mushy when cooked but will do in a pinch. Other good *Suillus* mushrooms are *S. grevillei* (larch bolete), *S. brevipes,* and *S. pictus*—a very pretty, heavily ornamented mushroom. The *S. luteus* has found its way into the important commercial market and in dried form is imported in significant quantities from Chile.

Mushrooms Krakow Style

To make this dish, you must use a rich extract from dried wild mushrooms. You may use fresh or even canned mushrooms, but if you use fresh ones they must first be blanched by covering them with water, bringing to a boil, then draining off the liquid.

Rinse and drain the blanched or canned mushrooms. Set aside.

Place the cèpes and onion in a medium saucepan and cover with 2 cups water. Bring to a boil and let the cèpes simmer for 30 minutes. Remove the onion and cèpes from the liquid and reduce the liquid to ⅓ cup. Add the salt, sugar, soy sauce, sherry, and all but ⅓ cup of the cream to the mushroom liquid. Keep warm over low heat.

Beat the eggs with the remaining cream until well blended. Add the drained mushrooms and cèpes to the saucepan, increase to medium heat, and while stirring continuously, slowly add the cream-egg yolk mixture. Continue stirring until it thickens, then remove from the heat and serve immediately in small warmed bowls with fresh bread.

Serves 4
Suggested wine: Kistler Chardonnay

---

2 cups blanched fresh mushrooms or 2 (8-ounce) cans wild mushrooms
⅓ ounce dried cèpes
½ cup chopped onion
1 teaspoon salt
1 teaspoon sugar
1 tablespoon soy sauce
½ teaspoon sweet sherry or Madeira
1½ cups heavy cream
4 egg yolks

Wild Mushroom Bread Sauce

This sauce is a coarse, bold, country concoction—very flavorful and satisfying. It can be made smooth, but that is not necessary—it depends on how you wish to use it. The addition of the bread for thickening makes this sauce unpredictable, but also is the source of its charm. I prefer to serve it lumpy, with not all of the bread crumbs absorbed. It is great with quail, rabbit, or chicken.

> *½ ounce dried cèpes*
> *½ teaspoon salt*
> *¼ teaspoon sugar*
> *1 teaspoon soy sauce*
> *Black pepper*
> *½ to ¾ cup fresh bread crumbs*
> *2 tablespoons butter (optional, but it makes a richer sauce)*

In a small saucepan, combine the mushrooms, salt, sugar, soy sauce, and pepper. Add 2 cups of water and bring to a boil. Simmer for 20 minutes over low heat. Strain the reconstituted mushrooms if you want a smooth sauce. If not, leave the mushrooms in the liquid.

Gradually add the bread crumbs and begin to stir into the sauce. The amount of crumbs that can be absorbed will depend on the type of bread you use. Start by adding ½ cup and stir well. Add more crumbs if necessary; you can always add a little water if the sauce gets too thick. (If you want a smooth sauce, puree in a blender or food processor, then add the mushrooms.) Stir in the butter until it melts. Serve immediately.

Makes 2 cups

Cèpe Oil

There are times when you want to impart a subtle mushroom flavor to a dish without intruding too much on the other flavors—a good time for a mushroom oil. In order to keep the subtle flavor, you must use a mild oil, such as safflower or sunflower, not olive oil.

> *1 ounce dried cèpes*
> *3 cups safflower or sunflower oil*

Place the mushrooms and oil in a container with a tight-fitting lid. Let sit for several weeks in a cool spot, until a noticeable change in color occurs. Do not let the oil sit where it is above 70° F. or it may become rancid. Cèpe oil will keep for several weeks or longer if refrigerated.

Makes 3 cups

Cream of Rice Soup with Curry, Cèpes, and Watercress

When I pureed my first batch of cooked rice for a soup, I discovered a wonderful, rich, creamy substance that lent a unique texture but had one drawback— it left a starchy residue in the mouth, even after the rice had been thoroughly washed. Moreover, the dried cèpes added additional body to the mixture. Still, I could not let go of this substance because of the magical, unctuous roundness it left in my mouth.

The solution was quite simple and involves a principle common to seasoning in general. Flavors that are big and ungainly in the mouth can be mitigated by the addition of an acid that "fools" the palate, in this case drawing attention away from the starchiness and toward the acidic sharpness. And no acidic solution works better than a puree that carries the flavor of a fresh green or herb, such as watercress. You may substitute any fresh herb. Other dried mushrooms can also be used, but none will give the intensity of cèpes. You will simply have a milder flavored soup.

---

1 cup basmati rice, rinsed well
¹/₂ ounce dried cèpes
1¹/₂ teaspoons salt
¹/₂ teaspoon sugar
2 tablespoons soy sauce
¹/₂ teaspoon roasted sesame oil
¹/₂ small onion, thinly sliced
2 teaspoons curry powder
1 teaspoon paprika
2 cups milk
3 tablespoons Red Pepper Puree (page 69)
Watercress Sauce (page 70)

Bring 5 cups of water to a boil in a large pot. Add the rice while stirring, bring back to a boil, then turn down to a simmer. Cover and cook for 30 minutes.

While the rice is cooking, place 2 cups of water in a small saucepan. Add the cèpes, salt, sugar, soy sauce, sesame oil, onion, curry powder, and paprika. Bring to a boil, then turn down the heat and simmer for 20 minutes.

Combine the cooked rice with its liquid, the mushroom mixture with its liquid, and the milk in a blender. Blend until smooth, adding more milk if necessary and adjusting for salt. Stir in the red pepper puree.

Put into bowls and swirl a teaspoon of watercress sauce in each.

Serves 4 to 6
Suggested wine: Sanford Pinot Noir

Wild Mushroom and Onion Soup

Traditional French onion soup needs no embellish-ments—except maybe this one. The dried cèpes add body and earthiness while maintaining a vegetarian simplicity. Dried shiitake make a different but intriguing variation. If you use dried shiitake, slice them after reconstitution.

Place the olive oil and butter in a large sauté pan over medium heat. Add the onions and slowly sauté, stirring occasionally. You want the onions to cook slowly without browning—as long as 30 minutes.

While the onions are cooking, combine the mushrooms with 4 cups of water and the salt, soy sauce, and sugar in a 2-quart saucepan.

3 tablespoons olive oil

2 tablespoons butter

4 medium onions, sliced

1 ounce dried cèpes, preferably sliced

1 teaspoon salt

1 tablespoon soy sauce

1/2 teaspoon sugar

8 slices Gruyère cheese

4 slices French bread, brushed with oil and toasted

Bring to a boil and then simmer until the onions are done.

Add the onions to the mushroom liquid and simmer for another 30 minutes. Preheat the oven to 350° F.

Place 2 slices of the cheese on top of each slice of toasted bread. Ladle about a cup of soup into each of 4 narrow-mouthed bowls. Float the bread on top of the soup and place in the oven for 6 to 10 minutes, until the cheese is melted. Serve immediately.

Serves 4
Suggested wine: Madeira

Calamari Soup with Wakame and Cèpes

This soup is very similar to dashi (see page 163), with two important differences. First, it is made with a different kind of seaweed, wakame not konbu, and dried mushrooms are used in the broth to create a new flavor that is of both the earth and the sea. You will find the flavor smoky and somewhat haunting.

Other dried mushrooms can be used here, but will give markedly different flavors. Dried oyster mushrooms are not recommended because they are really too mild to lend any flavor to this traditional broth.

Put some water in a 2-quart saucepan and bring to a boil. Lightly salt the water and add the squid. Remove the squid from the water when it returns to a boil. The squid should just begin to turn milky white. Drain the squid, plunge into icy water to stop the cooking, and discard the water.

Bring 4 cups of water to a boil and add the dried mushrooms and salt. Turn the heat down and simmer for 20 minutes. Lift the mushrooms out of the liquid and, when cooled, slice into ½-inch pieces. Set the mushrooms aside.

Wipe the wakame with a damp cloth. Add to the hot mushroom liquid and bring to a gentle simmer. Let simmer for 10 minutes, then strain through a sieve. Rinse the wakame well and slice into ½-inch-wide pieces. Set aside.

Add the bonito flakes to the cooking liquid and simmer for another 10 minutes. Strain the liquid through a sieve and discard the bonito residue.

Bring the liquid back to a simmer once more and add the sliced mushrooms, wakame, and squid. Let simmer for 5 minutes, then add the scallions and serve immediately.

Serves 4
Suggested wine: Chablis

> *2 medium squid, cleaned and sliced into ¼-inch rings*
>
> *½ ounce dried cèpes*
>
> *1 teaspoon salt*
>
> *½ ounce dried wakame (available in health food stores and Asian markets)*
>
> *½ ounce bonito flakes (available in health food stores and Asian markets)*
>
> *2 scallions, white part and 1 inch into the green part, thinly sliced*

Jellied Three-Mushroom Consommé

Any variety of dried mushroom can be used to make this consommé, but these three are generally available (black trumpets are sold in specialty stores, dried oyster mushrooms in Asian markets). You may substitute dried shiitake for the black trumpets, but you will not get the intense black color.

You will need 3 small saucepans. In each pan, place 2 cups water, one variety of dried mushroom, ¼ teaspoon of the sugar, ½ teaspoon of the salt, and 1 teaspoon of the soy sauce. Bring each pan to a boil and then simmer for 20 minutes. Strain the liquids through a fine sieve lined with cheesecloth. You should have a little more than 1 cup of each extract. Save the mushroom solids for making dux-elles (see page 98).

Return each extract to its saucepan. Add 2 tea-spoons of the gelatin to each of the pans, bring back to a light simmer, and stir until all the gelatin is dissolved.

Pour into 3 separate flat-bottomed pans 6 to 8 inches long and 4 to 5 inches wide. The tricky thing here is to find pans that are not warped on the bottom and that will allow the liquid to gel evenly. Place the 3 pans in the refrigerator and let cool for several hours or overnight.

Remove the jellied consommés from the refrigerator. Cut into squares and place several pieces of each in a large wine glass. Sprinkle with a mixture of chopped scallions and chopped parsley and serve.

Serves 4
Suggested wine: Dry sherry

½ ounce dried cèpes
½ ounce black trumpets
(Craterellus fallax)
½ ounce dried oyster mushrooms
¾ teaspoon sugar
1 ½ teaspoons salt
3 teaspoons soy sauce
6 teaspoons unflavored powdered gelatin
Chopped scallions
Chopped fresh parsley

Marinated and Grilled Cèpes

A few glasses of good wine, a warm summer night, and a breeze to keep the mosquitoes off bare arms are enough to begin a heated discussion on the right way to prepare mushrooms for grilling. One school contends that a simple coating of extra-virgin olive oil is sufficient; indeed, Italians often prepare huge caps of porcini (cèpes) in this manner. Others contend that some sharp cheese is necessary, while aficionados claim that herbed vinegar is necessary. Though I urge caution in the use of any acid in mushroom preparations, my preference tilts toward the latter approach. Large mushrooms in general are big expanses of nutty-buttery flavor and their character can come through very nicely even when seasoned with a good herbed wine vinegar. If your grill is very hot, you should turn the mushrooms once or twice during grilling, but don't worry about a little charring on the edge—it adds character. The interplay of grilled and buttery flavors with the tangy herbed marinade is what makes this such a satisfying dish.

Portobellos can be substituted, or even large domestic caps can be used.

This recipe can also be prepared in a 325° F oven for seven to nine minutes, depending on the size of the mushrooms. Some caps can be as wide as six inches across, and these require a full nine minutes.

If possible make the marinade a day ahead and let it sit in a cool place or in the refrigerator; let stand at room temperature for 30 minutes before using.

---

4 large-cap fresh cèpes

⅓ cup wine vinegar, preferably infused with savory

⅔ cup olive oil

½ teaspoon salt

½ teaspoon sugar

1 small onion, finely chopped

1 teaspoon minced garlic

Prepare a charcoal grill.

Clean the mushrooms and slice off the stems. Then slice the stems lengthwise because they are quite meaty and more dense than the caps.

Combine the vinegar, olive oil, salt, sugar, onion, and garlic in a large bowl and stir well so that the salt and sugar dissolve. Then add the mushroom caps and stems and let sit in the marinade for 15 minutes, basting frequently.

Remove the mushrooms from the marinade and grill for 3 to 4 minutes on each side, turning occasionally if the grill is very hot. Serve whole, with the stems placed back inside the caps.

Serves 4

Suggested wine: Monterey Peninsula Winery Chardonnay

Duck with Ginger, Raspberries, and Marinated Cèpes

I have a thing about duck. In many restaurants, after a hearty sigh, I have succumbed to what can only be described as a culinary addiction. "I'll have the duck" has become so commonplace that my wife doesn't even bother to roll her eyes anymore. So duck is on the menu at Joe's constantly, with new variations appearing every few months.

I am really excited about this preparation, which pairs a zingy sauce with marinated cèpes. I prefer using ground ginger rather than fresh in this recipe, but you must be sure that it is freshly ground. The finished sauce should have a noticeable heat to it, even though that heat will be much muted when the sauce is eaten with the duck.

Portobello mushrooms can be substituted for the cèpes. If possible, make the mushroom marinade a day ahead of time and let sit in a cool place or in the refrigerator; let it come to room temperature before

using. Also, it is best to let the duck come to room temperature before you sauté it.

THE MARINATED CÈPES
½ cup red or white wine vinegar

½ cup olive oil

1 tablespoon soy sauce

2 teaspoons sugar

1 small onion, finely chopped

1 teaspoon minced garlic

2 large fresh cèpe caps, cleaned

THE DUCK
Salt

4 single duck breasts, trimmed of excess fat

½ cup dry red wine

2 tablespoons sugar

1 tablespoon dark soy sauce

2 teaspoons ground ginger

1 teaspoon arrowroot mixed with ⅓ cup cold water

1 tablespoon pickled ginger, finely chopped (available in Asian markets)

½ cup fresh red raspberries

Combine the vinegar, olive oil, soy sauce, sugar, onion, and garlic in a bowl and stir until the sugar dissolves. Add the mushrooms and marinate for 15 minutes, basting frequently.

Preheat the oven to 325° F.

Remove the mushrooms from the marinade, place in a baking dish, and bake for 7 to 9 minutes, depending on their size. Set aside.

Lightly salt the duck breast all over, then pat dry. Place a large sauté pan over high heat. When very hot, add the duck breasts skin side down and cook for 6 minutes. Turn the breasts over, reduce the heat to medium, and cook for 3 minutes more. Then turn the duck over to its

(continued on page 98)

Duck with Ginger, Raspberries, and Grilled Cèpes

(continued from page 97)

skin side again and cook until the skin becomes dark brown, about 1 to 2 minutes. The duck should be medium-rare. Remove and keep warm.

In a small saucepan, combine the wine, sugar, soy sauce, and ginger. Add ½ cup water and bring to a boil. Simmer for 1 minute, then stir in the arrowroot mixture and heat gently until the sauce thickens.

Slice the cèpes and arrange on one side of the plate. Slice the duck and arrange it on the opposite side of the plate. Add the pickled ginger and raspberries to the sauce, pour over the duck, and serve.

Serves 4

Suggested wine: A cassis-style Cabernet Sauvignon from the Santa Cruz Mountains, such as Ridge, Santa Cruz Mountain Vineyard, or David Bruce

Duxelles from Dried Cèpes

There are many times when you might want a mushroom extract made from dried cèpes. Well and good, but what of the poor residual mushrooms, squeezed of their rich character? Happily, there is plenty of character left in them and they make wonderful duxelles. Use the duxelles to cover fish or meat or, better yet, as filling for ravioli or tortellini. Or wrap them in wonton skins and use in soup.

> 1½ tablespoons butter
> ⅓ cup chopped onion
> ½ ounce dried cèpes, reconstituted and chopped
> ½ teaspoon soy sauce
> ½ teaspoon salt
> ¼ teaspoon sugar

Place the butter and onion in a small sauté pan over medium heat. Sauté for 2 minutes. Add the mushrooms, soy sauce, salt, and sugar and continue to sauté for another 2 minutes. Let cool and refrigerate. The duxelles can be refrigerated for a week or frozen indefinitely.

Makes ⅓ cup

Mashed Potatoes with Cèpe Gravy and Truffled Bourbon

Serve this dish using slices of medium-rare beef or venison arranged around the potatoes as a garnish. The truffled bourbon is something you should keep on hand year-round. When available, you should buy some fresh truffles—Oregon white or black truffles, French black, or Italian white truffles. Slice the truffles and place them in a jar with a wide mouth so they will be easier to remove later. Cover the truffles completely with a good bourbon. The bourbon will take on the wonderful truffle character and is so much better in recipes that call for brandy.

Combine the cèpes, 2 cups of water, sugar, salt, and soy sauce in a small saucepan and bring to a boil, then let simmer for 20 minutes.

While the mushrooms are simmering, sauté the onion in the butter for 1 minute over medium heat and add the flour to make a roux. Stir together for 1 or 2 minutes, until the roux becomes lightly golden. Set aside.

Pour the mushrooms with their liquid over the roux and stir over medium heat until the mixture is thickened. Add the truffled bourbon along with some slices of the truffles to the sauce and heat for another 2 minutes.

In the center of each plate, mound some of the mashed potatoes and make a well in the center with a spoon. Pour in some of the sauce, then surround the potatoes with slices of beef or venison.

Serves 4
Suggested wine: Mount Eden Pinot Noir

½ ounce dried cèpes
½ teaspoon sugar
½ teaspoon salt
2 teaspoons soy sauce
1 tablespoon chopped onion
2 tablespoons butter
1 tablespoon flour
2 tablespoons truffled bourbon plus slices of the liquor-preserved truffles
4 medium potatoes, peeled, cooked, and mashed
Slices of beef or venison

Cèpe-Cabernet Pâté with Fresh Grape Sauce, Belgian Endive, and Pickled Mushrooms

This is one of my favorite recipes for fall, when Concord grapes are in season.

In a small saucepan, place the cèpes and cover with water. Bring to a boil, then simmer for 20 minutes.

Place ⅓ of the butter in a skillet and melt over medium heat. Sauté the garlic and onion until onion is limp, about 2 minutes. Push aside the onion and garlic and add the livers. Sauté on each side for about 3 minutes. Add the mushrooms with their liquid, the wine, and the cognac. Continue to stir and simmer until only about 1 tablespoon liquid is left in the pan. Let cool for 10 minutes.

Place the liver mixture in a food processor and process, adding the rest of the butter a sliver at a time. Remove the mixture from the processor and force through a fine sieve. It should be very smooth.

Butter, then line the bottom

THE PÂTÉ
¼ ounce dried cèpes or other dried mushrooms
½ cup butter
2 tablespoons chopped garlic
1 large onion, medium sliced
6 ounces chicken, duck, or goose livers
⅓ cup Cabernet Sauvignon
1 tablespoon cognac
Salt

THE GRAPE SAUCE
2 large bunches Concord grapes (or any other good red wine grapes, not the common seedless table variety), stems included
2 tablespoons sugar
Juice of 1 lemon
1 tablespoon cornstarch mixed with 1 tablespoon cold water

THE HABAÑERO SAUCE
4 habañero chiles (or any other hot variety, such as serrano), stems removed, seeded, sliced in half
1 teaspoon crushed garlic
⅓ cup finely chopped onion
1 teaspoon tomato paste
¼ teaspoon salt

THE ENDIVE
1 small Belgian endive, slivered and marinated (see recipe, page 164)
Pickled Straw Mushrooms (page 161)

of a 2-quart pâté pan or any narrow, shallow baking pan with waxed paper. Pour in the pâté mixture and place in the refrigerator. Chill until firm, about 3 hours, or overnight.

Place the ingredients for the grape sauce except the cornstarch mixture in a saucepan, mashing the grapes a bit to release some juice. Bring to a boil over medium heat, then cover and simmer for 45 minutes. This should release most of the juice from the grapes. Push the mixture through a fine sieve to extract all the liquid. Return the liquid to a small saucepan, bring to a simmer, and thicken by slowly adding the cornstarch mixture while stirring. The sauce should coat a spoon. Refrigerate the sauce until it is cold. This will thicken it further.

Combine the ingredients for the habañero sauce in a blender and puree until smooth. Set aside.

Cut the chilled pâté into 4 pieces, placing each in the

center of a large salad plate. Surround each piece with grape sauce to the rim. Dot the grape sauce with a little of the habanero sauce, and with a toothpick, connect all the dots through the grape sauce to create a design. Cover the pâté with the marinated endive and the pickled mushrooms and serve.

Serves 4
Suggested wine: Spottswoode Cabernet Sauvignon

Creamed Corn with Cèpes

Make this dish when corn is at the height of its season. The luscious sweetness of fresh corn dovetails dramatically with the earthy goodness of the dried cèpes.

It is a good side dish, and can also be served underneath slices of fresh duck or turkey breast.

Remove the corn kernels from the cobs with a knife. You should have about 2 cups of corn. Cream the corn by mincing it on a cutting board, or place in a food processor and pulse very quickly, wiping down the sides of the bowl with a rubber spatula. Avoid long continuous processing, which would make the corn too mushy.

Place the cèpes in small saucepan with 1 cup of water and the soy sauce. Bring to a boil and simmer for 20 minutes. Remove the mushrooms from the liquid and reduce the liquid to ¹⁄₃ cup. Chop the mushrooms finely and add to the reduced liquid. Add the corn and cream, stir together, and slowly heat the mixture while stirring so that it is just slightly bubbling. Season carefully with salt and serve.

Serves 4

> 4 ears fresh corn
> ¹⁄₂ ounce dried cèpes
> 2 teaspoons soy sauce
> ¹⁄₂ cup heavy cream
> Salt

My Mother's Baked Shad with Cèpe Butter

For all the dreariness associated with the month of February in eastern Pennsylvania, we always have the first shad of the season to look forward to. Peeling the paper off the carefully fileted fish and experiencing its heady aroma makes the rest of winter seem bearable. Accompany this baked shad with fresh asparagus, sautéed with lots of garlic.

Place the cèpes, soy sauce, and sugar in a small saucepan and add water to cover. Bring to a boil, then simmer for 20 minutes. Let cool. Place the mushrooms and liquid in a blender and puree until smooth. Whisk in the butter and refrigerate until ready to use.

Bring about 2 cups water to a boil in a medium saucepan. When boiling, add the shad roe and leave in the water until the water comes to a boil again, simmer 1 minute, then remove roe from the water, pat dry, and let rest for 10 minutes. Peel away any skin and sinew.

Place the roe in a large bowl and gently begin to break it up with a fork; do not grind or make the roe mushy. Add the butter, parsley, onion, and sherry and work in until the stuffing resembles a thin paste. Add the bread crumbs, then season with salt and pepper to taste.

Open the shad pieces so they are flat on your work surface. First, use the roe stuffing to fill in the area between the outer flaps and the center. Then fold the flaps back toward the center. Stuff the space left open near the top and smooth until the stuffing is even with the shad.

Lay each piece of stuffed shad on a piece of aluminum foil cut so that you can enclose it (about 12 by 12 inches). Lightly salt the shad, sprinkle a little sherry on each piece, and cut thin slivers of the hardened cèpe butter on top. Wrap the shad in the aluminum foil. (The shad can now be refrigerated and baked within a day or baked immediately.)

Preheat the oven to 450° F. Bake shad for 15 minutes. Unwrap, and carefully pour some of the cèpe butter back onto the filets. Serve immediately.

Serves 4
Suggested wine: A rich, woody Chardonnay, such as Kistler Vineyard

---

THE CÈPE BUTTER
¹/₄ ounce dried cèpes
1 teaspoon soy sauce
Pinch of sugar
¹/₃ cup softened butter

THE SHAD
1 medium shad roe, 5 to 6 ounces
¹/₂ cup butter, melted
1 tablespoon finely chopped fresh parsley
3 tablespoons finely chopped onion
2 tablespoons dry sherry, plus additional for sprinkling
1 cup fresh bread crumbs
Salt and pepper
4 small pieces boned shad, cut from whole boned side, skin on, 5 to 7 ounces each

Veal Diccalata

We usually hunt mushrooms in the woods surrounding Reading, Pennsylvania. However, because we live in a suburban area, we find them occasionally on lawns—especially near trees or recently removed trees. My father and mother moved out near our house a few years back when our youngest son, Stefan, was five. My father would climb into the Jeep with Stefan and off they would go in search of exotic fungi on the lawns of Wyomissing. More than once they found fungal gold. On one occasion, they discovered a mushroom that we had never found before, a bolete called Boletus appendiculatus. Stefan would be dispatched to retrieve the mushrooms, which were plentiful on lawns that summer, and when riding around and spotting the mushroom he would yell, "Pop-pop, Pop-pop! Diccalata! Diccalata!," his version of that mycological mouthful. So what else could I call this dish when I used these mushrooms? But I have been solemnly informed on at least one occasion by a food colleague that he knew the little village in Italy where this dish comes from. I like to serve it with Pennsylvania Polenta (page 166) and green beans with aïoli.

Because Boletus appendiculatus is available to only the most avid (and lucky) mushroom hunters, this recipe calls for dried cèpes.

---

4 veal chops, cut from the loin or rack

Salt

1/2 ounce dried cèpes

2 tablespoons chopped onion

2 tablespoons butter

1 teaspoon sugar

1 tablespoon soy sauce

Sautéed button mushroom slices (optional)

Preheat the oven to 450° F.

Arrange the chops on a rack or roasting pan and salt lightly. Place in the oven and roast for 15 to 20 minutes.

Place the cèpes and 2 cups water in a small saucepan. Bring the water to a boil and then simmer for 10 minutes.

While the mushrooms are simmering, sauté the onion in the butter until translucent, about 2 minutes.

Strain the mushroom liquid through a fine sieve and rinse the mushrooms thoroughly, then combine them with the liquid. Add the onion and 1 teaspoon salt, the sugar, and the soy sauce. Transfer to a blender and process until smooth. Return to the saucepan and reheat.

When chops are done, place on serving dishes and cover with the sauce. If desired, garnish with some sautéed thickly sliced button mushrooms.

Serves 4

Suggested wine: Big-bodied Petit Sirah, such as Guenoc

A Sauce from Dried Cèpes

My ancestors, the Poles, loved dried boletes. When I first smelled dried Polish cèpes—or borovicki, as they are known in Polish—in a plastic bag, I wanted to be a mushroom sniffer for the rest of my life. The dried form has an intense earthy aroma matched perhaps only by the truffle, another mycological aphrodisiac. This sauce is best with veal or pasta.

Dried cèpes usually come in ½- to 1-ounce packages, sliced. The much rarer Polish mushrooms can be found as whole caps. You must simmer the whole Polish mushrooms longer than the sliced ones, and you'll have to slice the mushrooms before use.

1 ounce dried cèpes
2 tablespoons chopped onion
2 tablespoons butter
1 teaspoon salt
1 teaspoon sugar
1 tablespoon soy sauce
2 teaspoons arrowroot mixed in ⅓ cup cold water

Place the cèpes and 3 cups of water in a medium saucepan and bring to a boil over medium heat. Let simmer for 20 minutes.

Meanwhile, in a large skillet sauté the onion in the butter until translucent, about 2 minutes.

Add the cèpes and their liquid, salt, sugar, and soy sauce. Reduce to 2 cups. Strain the liquid through a fine sieve, then place in the saucepan over medium heat. Add the arrowroot mixture and stir until thickened. Return the mushrooms to the sauce and use immediately.

Serves 4

Quick Wild Mushroom Soup

Combine the cèpes and 4 cups of water in a 2-quart saucepan and bring to a boil. Let simmer for 20 minutes. Let cool for 5 minutes, then strain liquid. Puree mushrooms and liquid in a blender. Return the puree to the saucepan and add the onion powder, salt, sugar, butter, and

1 ounce dried cèpes
2 teaspoons onion powder
1 teaspoon salt
½ teaspoon sugar
4 tablespoons butter, melted
2 tablespoons soy sauce
Crème fraîche

soy sauce. Stir and simmer for 5 minutes. Ladle into soup bowls and spread a dab of crème fraîche over the top of each serving, then serve immediately.

Serves 4
Suggested wine: Chardonnay

Winter Borscht

Beet soup—known more commonly by its Eastern European name, borscht—is often made with dried wild mushrooms to give the soup more body. This recipe takes that idea one step further by pureeing the beets with the mushrooms, thus making a thick, rich soup in which the mushrooms enliven the beets.

Fresh beets can also be used here, but must be cooked until tender and the juice retained.

> *¹/₂ ounce dried cèpes*
> *1 (16-ounce) can sliced beets*
> *1 teaspoon onion powder*
> *2 tablespoons sugar*
> *Juice of 1 lemon*
> *¹/₄ teaspoon black pepper*
> *Sour cream*

Place the mushrooms in a 2-quart saucepan and add 3 cups of water. Bring to a boil and simmer for 15 minutes.

Remove a few of the mushrooms from the saucepan and slice thin. Strain the liquid, then add the rest of the mushrooms and liquid to a blender. Add the beets along with the juice. Process until smooth.

Return the puree to the saucepan, turn the heat to low, and add the onion powder, sugar, lemon juice, and black pepper. Stir with a whisk and simmer over low heat for 5 minutes. Pour the soup into mugs, add a dollop of sour cream, and top with the sliced cèpes before serving.

Serves 4
Suggested wine: Ridge Zinfandel

Cèpe Risotto

For the pure enjoyment of the flavor of cèpes, this risotto is hard to beat. The key to this recipe is to stop cooking the risotto before it is completely done and let it stand for 5 to 10 minutes before serving.

> *2 ounces dried cèpes*
> *5 cups veal stock or chicken stock*
> *Salt*
> *6 tablespoons lightly salted butter*
> *¹/₂ cup finely chopped onions*
> *1 cup Arborio rice*
> *¹/₃ cup grated Parmesan cheese*

Place the cèpes and the stock in a small saucepan. Bring to a boil and let simmer for 20 minutes. Strain the liquid through a coffee filter into a clean saucepan. Add enough water to make 5 cups of liquid. Add salt until the liquid tastes like a light soup, but no more. Keep simmering over low heat.

Remove the cèpes from the filter, rinse them, and chop finely.

Place the butter in a large saucepan over medium heat. Add the onion and sauté for 1 minute. Add the chopped cèpes and the rice and stir for 30 seconds. Add 1 cup of the stock and stir until the liquid has been absorbed by the rice, then add another cup of stock and continue stirring. Continue adding stock in 1 cup amounts until most of the liquid has been absorbed, in 30 to 40 minutes. Taste the rice. It should be just a little firm in the middle. Cover and let stand off the heat for 5 to 10 minutes, then sprinkle the Parmesan over the top and serve.

Serves 4

Workman's Omelet

This mushroom omelet is an original creation dedicated to my publisher. It is also a hearty rendition of an American classic.

Place the cèpes in a small saucepan. Cover with water, bring to a boil, and let simmer for 20 minutes. Remove the mushrooms from the liquid, and reduce liquid to 1 to 2 tablespoons. Let the liquid cool. While the liquid is cooling finely chop the cèpes and set aside.

Place the butter in a 6-inch nonstick sauté pan over medium heat and sauté the onion for 1 minute. Add the sliced button mushrooms and continue to sauté until they have given off their liquid and the liquid has evaporated, about 10 minutes. Add the cèpes and season mixture with salt.

In a separate bowl, combine the eggs with the cooled cèpe liquid and whip well with a whisk. You may add a little cream at this point if you wish.

Place the mushroom-filled skillet over medium-low heat, stir, and slowly add the eggs. Stir until eggs and mushrooms are combined. Let cook over low heat until the eggs begin to set along the edges, about 1 minute. Sprinkle the cheese over the skillet, flip half the omelet over the other half, remove from the heat, and serve immediately.

Makes 1 omelet

---

¹⁄₄ ounce dried cèpes
2 tablespoons butter
¹⁄₃ cup thinly sliced onion
²⁄₃ cup sliced button mushrooms
Salt
3 eggs
Heavy cream (optional)
¹⁄₃ cup grated Romano cheese

Chanterelle

FLOWER OR FUNGUS?

Chanterelles

FOR ANYONE GROWING UP IN A FAMILY of mushroom hunters, whiplash—caused by sudden braking at high speed on a busy road—is a fact of life. I remember several severe episodes during the summer of 1975, when Heidi and I, with my mother and father, decided to take a trip to Nova Scotia to go mushroom hunting. Now my father has never been known for dawdling on a highway when he wants to get from one place to another, and the scenery along the Canadian Coastal Highway was zipping by like a travel video on fast forward. Instead of trying to take it all in, Heidi and I settled in for a little nap. All of a sudden we felt a tremendous pull and jerk and heard the screech of rubber skidding on asphalt. We thought we had almost hit a moose when we noticed Pop pulling off onto the shoulder. We saw him peering intently out his window into a dark expanse of Canadian hardwoods. And then we all saw it. Twinkling in the depths of the black, moist, sylvan landscape were hundreds of orange points of light, like multiple Mars' glistening on a moonless night. As our eyes became adjusted, the lights took on definition and enlarged to reveal shapes reminiscent of tiger lilies, yet they were brighter and more vibrant—chanterelles. Against the rich darkness of the soil they shone like flowers displaying their golden radiance.

We have left good rubber on the highways of North America during such sightings. And how could we not? How could I go on when I saw the familiar shapes of mushrooms? This is the legacy of my father, who taught me all I know about mushroom hunting. But of all the sightings from all those roads in all those years, the most dramatic was the chanterelles of Nova Scotia.

Among the most widely picked wild mushrooms in the world, chanterelles may also be the most beloved. They symbolize happiness and abundance in the mycological world, and on the tables of families fortunate enough to recognize and enjoy them. In addition to having a distinct apricotlike flavor, they really do resemble flowers more than mushrooms. They are one of the few edible species that does not camouflage itself against its background and thus are easy to spot in a forest. Not that chanterelles grow everywhere. I can remember many summer afternoons in July, under perfect conditions, when we hunted for hours only to return with empty baskets. But when you do find chanterelles, there are likely to be many more nearby. Again, like flowers, they are gregarious and abundant given the right soil and weather conditions. In wet years we have picked bushels in an hour, moving from spot to spot on knees and bellies. The same is true for black chanterelles, which, though much smaller, grow in even larger numbers than golden chanterelles.

As a group, the chanterelles are a strikingly beautiful collection of forest ornaments. In eastern Pennsylvania they grow in deciduous forests from July through September.

Varieties of Chanterelles

"Chanterelle" refers both to the mushroom known as the golden chanterelle and to other closely related species. Thus it is a common name both for a mushroom (actually, several mushrooms) and a group of mushrooms related to the main type. Over the years, as the result of numerous mycological symposiums, some of these related species have been moved to or been reclassified into other genera. Still, the group commonly known as "the chanterelle group" remains intact and are discussed together in this chapter. There are enough similarities to warrant this approach, and also enough differences to discuss their characters separately.

Cantharellus cibarius, Cantharellus lateritius, Cantharellus odoratus Common name—chanterelle, golden chanterelle, *girolle, Pfifferling,* egg mushroom, *galinachi, shibatake.* This composes what we commonly know as the chanterelle, although, as you can see, there are three species that are distinct enough to merit separate scientific names. Practically, however, they are close enough to be discussed together and their culinary characteristics are similar. Chanterelles of this group all are dull to bright orange and very visible in the forest, although they are much brighter in the presence of moisture or after a heavy rain, which seems to revive them. In dry conditions, they lose their luster and are hard to see among leaves in the forest. The "true" chanterelle, *C. cibarius,* is plentiful on the West Coast and is by far the meatiest of the group. I have picked this mushroom in southern California, where just the very top was visible and the rest of the mushroom, fully developed, was below ground. Fully mature chanterelles can become quite large, growing to six inches high and weighing close to half a pound, but the typical specimen is usually three to five inches high from root to cap and quite firm. *C. lateritius* is much more common than *C. cibarius* in eastern North America and is generally a smaller, more delicate mushroom that spreads more over the ground than *C. cibarius.* It never weighs more than a few ounces and does not have the stature of *C. cibarius,* but it does have a very attractive tendency to appear like a bunch of flowers strewn along the forest floor. Also, its gill structure is much less defined than *C. cibarius* and even appears to be smooth on the underside of the cap, where *C. cibarius* has well defined ridges there. *C. odoratus* is similar to *C. lateritius* and is typified by a very fragrant aroma, which puts some people off. That aroma, similar to all three in somewhat different degrees, is of woodsy apricot, and that is what makes the chanterelle so popular. It is one of the few mushrooms that can be paired with lemon juice or another citric element and not lose its character. In fact, I like to use onions, butter, and chopped dried apricot when braising chanterelles. Otherwise, avoid strong competing flavors, such as garlic or spices, when cooking with chanterelles; fresh herbs, such as lemon thyme, can be used in moderation. The stems of the freshly picked mushrooms are more fibrous than the caps, but not considerably so. They just take a little more cooking time. Generally, however, you may cook the stems and caps together. I find chanterelles best paired with game or shellfish; Gewürztraminer or Riesling are great wine accompaniments. Chanterelles are also good candidates for pickling to use later in salads. I do not recommend drying them because the resulting liquid from reconstitution is disappointing. However, soaking dried chanterelles in vodka for a month yields an interesting essence for sauces. Chanterelles are best preserved by canning in jars.

Craterellus cornucopioides, Craterellus fallax, Craterellus cinereus   Common name—black chanterelles, horn-of-plenty, *Totentrompete, trompette du mort,* false truffle, poor man's truffle. This group of dark brown to black chanterelles goes by a series of names. For instance, *C. cornucopioides* usually goes by the name horn of plenty, while *C. fallax* is commonly called the black trumpet and *C. cinereus* is the black chanterelle. There is yet another, *C. foetidus,* that is called the fragrant black trumpet. There is some controversy over the relative quality of the *C. cinereus* and *C. foetidus,* which is a good example of disputes that can go on between mycologists and mycophagists. Upon browsing through my sources on these mushrooms, I found one author who rated *C. cinereus* "edible and delectable" while another grouped it with a look-alike, nonedible set of black mushrooms. On *C. foeditus,* the first author found it had a "sickly sweet odor," while the second found it "intensely satisfying, rivaled by no other mushroom." So much for unanimity among scientific sources. The vast majority of black chanterelles found commercially in North America—and from Europe and elsewhere—are of the first two varieties. They have taken on similarly grim names—*trompette du mort* in France, *Totentrompete* in Germany, and simply *trumpet of death* here. There is one more name that is not used much now but was once popular, the false truffle, because specks of this mushroom could resemble specks of real truffles in a dish. There is no similarity of flavor, but a chef wishing to impress a patron might substitute one for the other to get the same visual effect, and one would presume the heftier price. Thus poor man's truffle is also occasionally used, although poor chef's truffle might be more appropriate. Whatever you call it, this is one of my favorite mushrooms for cooking. Not only is it great fresh, with a buttery woodsy flavor, but unlike regular chanterelles it can also be successfully dried and reconstituted without loss of character. In fact, reconstituting the black chanterelle in water yields a dark, satiny liquid that looks gorgeous as a sauce for fish. Once dried, these mushrooms can also be powdered and used as a flavoring agent for sauces and soups. They can be pickled, but the best preservation, by far, is drying.

Cantharellus cinnabarinus   Common name—red chanterelle, cinnamon chanterelle, cinnabar-red chanterelle. This is one of the prettiest mushrooms on the forest floor in mid-summer. The caps rarely get larger than an inch across the top and are more frequently less than half that size. They seem to flow in quantity over the slopes of well-drained hillsides, where they reappear for years and years. Bright red in color, they lose little of it even when dry. We sprinkle a few of them raw over salads in our restaurant to perk up the greens because they have a pleasant peppery character. Use only fresh, because they do not dry well nor respond to any other form of preservation.

Cantharellus infundibulformis   Common name—funnel chanterelle, yellow-footed chanterelle, winter chanterelle, trumpet chanterelle. This is actually another group of the *Cantharellus* genus that has many common characteristics so can be discussed together. They are broken into *C. tubarformis* (trumpet), *C. xanthopus* (yellow-footed), and *C. minor* (small chanterelle). I call these mushrooms the "chop suey" chanterelles because the caps are so water-logged that when cooked they lose that water very quickly while the stems retain most of their shape. What you get in the pan is something that looks like chop suey. The flavor is not bad, but not particularly distinct, and although they are in the same genus as the classic chanterelle, they really are not a substitute for it. They cannot be successfully canned, so drying is the only method of preservation. They are distributed by wild mushroom wholesalers on the West Coast, primarily because they come up when there are few other species available. Still, they are pleasant-tasting mushrooms if you can't get anything else.

Cantharellus subalbidus   Common name—white chanterelle. Very similar to the classic chanterelle and a good substitute for it, except that it is much rarer. A real find for wild mushroom hunters, it can be prepared the same was as golden chanterelle.

Gomphus clavatus   Common name—pig's ears. A very funny-looking mushroom resembling a sawed-off purplish club, it nonetheless has culinary qualities worth noting, such as a firmness that many mushrooms lack. It generally retains this texture during cooking and is a welcome addition to any casserole, even though the flavor is not distinct.

Polyozellus multiplex   Common name—blue chanterelle, clustered blue chanterelle. Rarely found in the East, and generally rare in the United States except in the Rocky Mountains, this mushroom can grow to be quite large and is considered good eating—if not particularly exciting. It is spectacularly blue among thousands of species of mushrooms hued in earth tones.

In late July a few years back, I got a call from food personality Martha Stewart, who asked if she could go mushroom hunting with us; she was doing a story on mushrooms for her magazine. I told her it was fine provided the mushrooms cooperated, but that we hadn't had rain for a few weeks and I really couldn't promise anything. She said she'd take her chances, so we set a date.

As the day approached I became increasingly apprehensive because there had still been no rain. All of our favorite spots were barren, with nothing but dry polypores around dead trees to represent the fungal world. It was depressing and I decided to call and postpone our trip. But I got my dates mixed up and all of a sudden she was here. I thought we could scrape off some wood fungus and illustrate how they could be used as toothpicks, but we went out into the woods anyway. After about an hour we drove to a spot where we had picked chanterelles the year before, hoping against hope that we might find something. When I was up on the trail, several people including my children—Chris, Sonja, Stefan, and Martha—began to chatter excitedly. There on one of the lower paths was a patch of about twenty worn but living chanterelles. We gathered around and for the next few hours took thousands of pictures from every angle. The hunt was a success.

As we walked away from that patch of chanterelles on that parched summer afternoon I couldn't help but marvel, as I glanced over my shoulder once more, at how those few mushrooms had sprung up out of nowhere under the worst possible conditions, just to get their picture taken. With just a twinge of pique, I returned and picked them for supper.

Those were the last mushrooms we found that year.

Salmon with Chanterelles and Red Pepper Puree

With their ability to mix and match with acidic foods, chanterelles are among the most versatile of wild mushrooms. This dish can be made with other fish, but works best with an oily fish, such as salmon and mackerel. Yellow or orange peppers make an interesting variation.

Preheat the oven to 350° F.

Place the peppers in a baking dish and put in the oven. Roast for 10 to 12 minutes. The skin will shrivel and begin to blacken in spots. Let cool in a paper bag. Remove the skin from the peppers, then slit the peppers open and remove the stem, seeds, and veins.

Place the peppers in a blender and add the lemon juice, sugar, and salt. Blend to a smooth puree. Place puree in a small saucepan and warm slightly.

2 large red bell peppers
3 tablespoons fresh lemon juice
1 tablespoon sugar
½ teaspoon salt
2 tablespoons olive oil
½ small onion, sliced
6 ounces fresh chanterelles, cleaned and sliced
4 salmon filets, 6 ounces each

Place the oil in a sauté pan over medium heat. Add the onion and sauté for 1 minute. Add the chanterelles, reduce the heat, cover, and cook for 10 minutes, adding a little water if the bottom of the pan is too dry.

Meanwhile, prepare the salmon by grilling 4 minutes on each side, lightly simmering for 30 minutes, or baking on a lined baking sheet in a 350° F. oven for 12 to 15 minutes. When the salmon is done, place some of the red pepper puree in the middle of each plate. Cover the puree with some of the mushrooms, place the salmon filets on top, and serve.

Serves 4
Suggested wine: Kunde Zinfandel

Tossed Mesclun Salad with Mustard Vinaigrette and Cinnamon Chanterelles

In late June, as spring turns into summer, I begin to check a small hillside where every year tiny Cantharellus cinnabarinus *grow. In dry years, they can be a very pale orange or even pink, while in wet years they are a proud and fiery red-orange. Some caps are not much larger than pinheads, while others reach the gigantic proportions of one inch across. In any case, it is a time of exhausting but satisfying picking because these are among the prettiest mushrooms in a summer forest.*

This mushroom can safely be eaten raw in small quantities and gives any salad a nice zing because of its peppery taste.

You can use any salad mixture you like, as well as your favorite salad dressing. But note that heavy, creamy dressings mask this mushroom too much.

---

¹/₄ cup red wine vinegar

¹/₂ cup good olive oil

1¹/₂ teaspoons salt

1 tablespoon sugar

1 teaspoon black pepper

¹/₄ teaspoon minced garlic

1¹/₂ tablespoons Dijon mustard

2 to 3 ounces mixed salad greens (mesclun mix is ideal)

¹/₂ cup fresh cinnamon chanterelles, cleaned

In a blender or food processor, combine the vinegar, olive oil, salt, sugar, pepper, garlic, and mustard to make the dressing. Toss this dressing with the salad greens, arrange on plates, and distribute the chanterelles over the tops of the salads.

Serves 4

Yellow-Footed Chanterelles with Ramps

As the winter breaks and spring begins in field and forest, the first of nature's bounty make themselves available for the table. Ramps, or wild leeks, are redolent of garlic and, although small, pack a big wallop of flavor. Scallions or regular leeks can be used in this dish, but you will have to add some garlic to approach the same effect.

Black chanterelles can also be used.

> *4 ounces ramps*
>
> *3 tablespoons butter*
>
> *10 thin slices fresh ginger or 1 teaspoon ground ginger*
>
> *14 ounces fresh yellow-footed chanterelles, well rinsed*
>
> *Soy sauce*
>
> *Salt*
>
> *Sugar*
>
> *1 teaspoon cornstarch mixed with 1 tablespoon water*

Cut off the roots of each ramp, then cut off the ramp where the white ends and the leafy part begins. (The leafy part can be used in salads, but must be thoroughly washed first.)

Place the butter in a large sauté pan over medium heat. Add the ramps and ginger and sauté for 1 minute over medium-high heat. Add the mushrooms and continue to sauté for 3 to 4 minutes. These mushrooms yield a lot of liquid while cooking; continue to cook until about a third of the liquid has cooked away. Season to taste with soy sauce, salt, and sugar. Stir in the cornstarch mixture and heat until it thickens before serving.

Serves 4

Suggested wine: Mirassou Chenin Blanc

Chanterelles with Orange Fritters

Hedgehog mushrooms could be sub-
stituted for the chanterelles.

Place the butter in a large sauté
pan over medium heat. Sauté the
onion for 30 seconds, then add
the mushrooms. Sauté until the
mushrooms begin to go limp,
about 3 minutes. Add the lemon
juice and sugar, stir, and season
with salt to taste. Keep warm.

   Heat the oil to 375° F. In a
bowl, combine the egg, milk,
cream, 2 tablespoons of water,
the sugar, a pinch of salt, and

4 tablespoons butter

1 small onion, chopped

12 ounces fresh chanterelles,
cleaned and sliced

1 teaspoon lemon juice

1 teaspoon sugar

Salt

2 quarts vegetable oil,
for frying

1 egg

1 tablespoon milk

1 tablespoon heavy cream

3 tablespoons confectioners' sugar

1/2 cup all-purpose flour

8 round slices of navel orange,
1/2 inch thick, rind left on

flour. Blend well with a whisk.
Dip the orange slices in the batter and place, 2 to 3 at a time,
in the oil. Fry until the fritters
are light golden, about 30 seconds. Remove and drain on a
plate lined with a paper towel.

   Place 2 fritters on each
serving plate, cover with
the chanterelles, and serve
immediately.

Serves 4
Suggested wine: Pine Ridge
Chenin Blanc

Curried Brandade with Black Trumpets

Brandade—a puree of salt cod with garlic, cream, and olive oil—is popular in Provence. This is a spicier version with curry and jalapeños topped off with flavored black trumpets. It is served hot or cold. Hot, it can be scooped up with toast points, while cold it is a great filling for cherry tomatoes as an hors d'oeuvre. This recipe is for the cold version, with a variation for the hot version.

Cover the cod completely with water and set aside in a cool place for 24 hours. During the soaking, change the water 3 or 4 times.

When ready to make the brandade, drain and place the cod in a large saucepan and cover with water. Bring water to a boil slowly, then turn off the heat, cover, and let cod sit for 10 minutes.

While cod is steeping, prepare the dried black trumpets. Place the mushrooms in a 1-quart saucepan and cover with 1 cup water. Add salt and soy sauce. Bring to a boil over medium heat and gently simmer for 10 minutes. The mushrooms should taste lightly flavored with the soy sauce. Remove from heat, pour off the liquid

> *1 pound salt cod*
> *½ ounce dried black trumpets, cleaned*
> *½ teaspoon salt*
> *½ teaspoon soy sauce*
> *⅓ cup coarsely chopped fennel*
> *¼ cup coarsely chopped fresh jalapeño or serrano chile*
> *1 tablespoon minced garlic*
> *2 teaspoons curry powder*
> *⅔ cup olive oil*
> *½ cup heavy cream*
> *30 cherry tomatoes, hollowed out and drained*

and reserve for another use, and cool the mushrooms in the refrigerator.

Drain the water from the cod and flake the fish with a fork. Taste the fish. It should have good flavor without being overly salty. If it is too salty, you will have to soak the flaked cod for an additional 30 minutes.

When cod is ready, place in a food processor and add the fennel, chile, garlic, and curry powder. Begin processing. Add the oil, a little at a time, alternating with the heavy cream until all the liquid is incorporated. The mixture should have the consistency of coarse mashed potatoes.

Pipe the brandade into the tomatoes, and top each with a piece of black trumpet. Serve.

Variation: To make a hot brandade, gently heat the mixture in a large double boiler. Stir frequently until the mixture is hot (about 30 to 45 minutes) and spread evenly into a shallow serving dish. Decorate with fresh herbs and scoop out onto toasted pita bread pieces or toast points.

Makes 30 hors d'oeuvres

Soft-Shell Crabs with Chanterelles

Eating soft-shell crabs is one of my favorite indulgences. The key to making the taste of these crabs so dramatic is to sauté them in lemon butter. It's different from simply squeezing lemon juice over already finished crabs. The play of the sweet crabmeat against the citric zing in the mouth makes this a thrilling culinary experience. Chanterelles are perfect with soft-shells because they are one of the few mushrooms that go well with lemony flavors.

Soft-shell crabs are available from May through September on the East Coast. They appear intermittently and sometimes with long gaps in between, so grab them when you see them.

Clean the crabs. Begin by cutting the eyes off, then pull off the small flap on the underside. Turn the crabs over and squeeze out the yellow bile under the top of the soft shell. Finally, rinse the crabs to wash away any remaining bile.

Combine the melted butter and lemon juice and place one fourth of the mixture in a nonstick sauté pan over medium heat. Sauté the chanterelles in the lemon butter for 2 to 3 minutes. Remove the mushrooms and keep warm.

Place the flour in a shallow dish. Lightly salt the flour and mix well. Dredge the crabs in the flour until they are well coated on both sides.

Add some more of the lemon butter to the pan and heat. Add the floured crabs, 2 at a time, and sauté for 2 to 3 minutes on each side. The flour will form a crust on the crabs. The crust should be brown with specks of black. You may have to adjust the heat to control this process. Remove crabs and place on a dish lined with paper towels to drain any residual butter and keep warm.

When the crabs are all sautéed, place on a serving dish, top with the chanterelles, and serve.

Serves 4
Suggested wine: Pouilly Fuissé

---

8 live soft-shell crabs
⅔ cup butter, melted
⅓ cup fresh lemon juice
2 cups whole small chanterelles, cleaned
1 to 2 cups all-purpose flour
Salt

Hen-of-the-Woods

MUSHROOMS FROM WOOD

The Ultimate Recyclers

As with other forms of nature, mushrooms live and grow within the dynamic of their environment. But, like some other natural forms, they cannot make the upward journey through the soil on their own. Mushrooms lack chlorophyll and cannot make their food, as do green plants. So, besides requiring rain, mushrooms need the food and nutrients that they glean from other elements in order to develop and grow. Those nutrients are different for each species of mushroom, but most often come from dead or dying trees.

Mushrooms break down complex organic compounds of trees into simpler forms that can then be used by plants for food. Thus their activity opens the door to new life, making available the building blocks for new compounds. Without mushrooms and fungi, the forest would die of hunger. A raspberry bush cannot consume a tree whole. It is the role of the fungi to recycle that which is complex and cumbersome into something simple and palatable for other living forms in this world.

The relationship between trees and mushrooms is what keeps both of their life cycles on the move. Indeed, trees and mushrooms share three main kinds of relationships: first, many fungi but relatively few mushrooms are parasitic, which means that the fungi feed off of living organisms—in this instance, trees. Honey mushrooms, for example, are parasitic under certain conditions. Other mushrooms live off the roots of trees. Some parasitize other mushrooms and change their character altogether; lobster mushrooms *(Hypomyces lactifluorum)* are the most famous. In all these instances, the fungus or mushroom grows at the expense of the living organism and signals the beginning of that organism's return to its basic compounds.

Second, some fungi live on matter already dead or decaying. This relationship is termed saprophytic and accounts for the growth of mushrooms on everything from dead wood to dung. Many more mushrooms fall into this group.

Third, some mushrooms and fungi grow in a mycorrhizal association with the roots of plants, most of which are trees. This is a symbiotic relationship in which the mushroom and tree derive benefits from each other. The mycelia (vegetative primary form of fungi lying underground) of the fungi often wrap in a sheathlike formation around the rootlets of the trees. This sheath aids the roots in absorbing nutrients such as phosphorus and other minerals as well as protecting the roots from certain diseases. In turn, the rootlets provide the fungi with moisture and many compounds—such as carbohydrates—that are vital for fungal growth and even for fruiting into mushrooms. Without these trees the mushrooms could not grow. In fact, it has been shown that trees deprived of their guests cannot compete successfully against other trees in the same area that have their fungal friends intact.

Most mushrooms that we pick and enjoy are mycorrhizal and are associated with specific trees, so a mushroom hunter should also be something of a tree expert. Some trees will support many kinds of fungi and thus are potential locations for mushroom fruitings. So you see that many mushrooms exist in a living environment with their hosts in that most beautiful of embraces—a symbiotic marriage.

Most mushrooms seem to pop right out of the ground from which they grow. It is not always easy to see that the mushroom comes from a mycelial system associated with a tree that is maybe yards away from the spot of fruiting: it looks like it has sprung up from the center of the earth. Other mushrooms, however, are more closely associated with the wood itself, even growing right out of that wood or in a bed of wood chips and mulch. These mushrooms are the subject of this chapter.

Varieties of Wood Mushrooms

Wood mushrooms fall into two broad groups: fleshy mushrooms that have a characteristic stalk and cap and look like any other mushroom; and polypores, which have amorphous shapes that do not resemble the general idea of mushrooms at all. The latter includes several species that have more in common with the tree from which they grew than with other mushrooms.

Note: There are varieties, such as shiitake, that grow directly out of wood but are so closely associated with Asian mushroom production that they have been included in the chapter on Asian mushrooms. There are also a few obscure species that are included in the general chapter covering commonly picked wild mushrooms.

The following mushrooms are either cultivated or capable of commercial cultivation.

Oyster Mushroom Group *Pleurotus ostreatus* Common name—oyster mushroom, oyster shelf, tree oyster, straw mushroom (also the name for *Volvariella volvaiacia*), *hiratake, tamogitake. Pleurotus porrigens* Common name—angel wings (also known as *Pleurocybella porrigens*). *Pleurotus citrinopileatus* Common name—golden oyster, *il'mak* (also referred to as *P. cornucopiae*). *Pleurotus cystidiosus* Common name—abalone mushroom, maple oyster mushroom, miller's oyster mushroom. *Pleurotus djamor* Common name—pink oyster mushroom, salmon oyster mushroom, strawberry oyster, flamingo mushroom, *takiiro hiratake. Pleurotus eryngii* Common name—king oyster. *Pleurotus euosmus*

Common name—tarragon oyster mushroom. *Pleurotus pulmonarius* Common name—Indian oyster, the phoenix. (Often called *Pleurotus sajor-caju,* the name most used by cultivators. Apparently *sajor-caju* is a misnomer owing to some taxonomical confusion. The real *sajor-caju* is now considered to be in the genus *Lentinus.* However, what cultivators call *sajor-caju* is really *P. pulmonarius.*)

If popularity is defined by the extent to which a species and subspecies have risen over a relatively short period of time, then this group must be the most popular mushroom of all time. A few years back the term *Oyster* defined a single mushroom on the market. Even though from its inception there have been several species on the market, the current variety of a single mushroom type is mind-boggling. What is even more impressive is that these oyster mushrooms, despite being in the same genus, can have significant differences in flavor and texture. You should know, however, that only a limited number of species are available at any time. Almost nobody grows all these species in the United States, and this expanded cultivation is at a nascent stage.

Although *Pleurotus* grow primarily on wood in the wild, they have been termed aggressive in their ability to sprout almost anywhere. David Arora, a mushroom expert on the West Coast, has a picture of *Pleurotus* growing out of a chair in his book, *Mushrooms Demystified.* They are so easy to grow and so efficient in their yield that they could be a candidate to reduce hunger in developing nations as well as a way to jump-start flagging agricultural economies. Oyster mushrooms are unusual in that they are members of one of the few genera that contain vitamin C as well as minerals and protein. They also contain a great quantity of free amino acids. Methods and substrates in cultivation account for wide variability in those properties, however. Detrimental factors include its relatively short shelf life and susceptibility to fly infestation, but these factors are being dealt with very aggressively and this mushroom should continue to be a popular domestic genus.

P. ostreatus is the first and best known of the group, and is the one you will most likely encounter in the forest. Many people think the wild version is best and I agree. It is usually meatier and has a more distinct flavor. The domestic version is also considered excellent, being surpassed only by *P. eryngii. P. citrinopileatus* has a lovely golden color with a noticeable citrus flavor and it is sometimes bitter. The most spectacular looking of this group or of any domestic mushroom is the *P. djamor,* which is a bright pink when raw. The color is lost on cooking, a downside to all the brightly colored mushrooms of this genus. I consider the taste of *Pleurotus* to be fairly mild compared to many of the wild species and the shiitake. It is a versatile mushroom and can be used in a variety of dishes, such as stir-fries. The stem is usually edible, if a little firmer than the cap. *Pleurotus* cannot be successfully pickled and, although sold dried, they are pretty useless in that form except as a last-minute addition to stews.

Stropharia rugoso-annulata Common name—king stropharia, garden giant, Burgundy mushroom, wine caps, wine red stropharia, Godzilla mushroom. The first reaction of anyone who has seen a sudden outcropping of these mushrooms in a garden is "wow!" We usually get emergency calls from friends who notice them growing in great profusion and to great size. It indeed looks as though Godzilla is wreaking havoc upon the earth when these benign creatures appear, sometimes growing to five or more pounds apiece. They are great grilled after painting with some oyster sauce or chipotle puree. They can be prepared the same way as portobellos. When you have young caps, they can be used in cream sauces, but once the caps open the mushrooms will darken anything to which they are added. Not a good mushroom for preserving, enjoy these from the ground directly into the pot!

Grifola frondosa Common name—hen-of-the-woods, ram's head, sheep's head, dancing butterfly mushroom, *maitake, kumotake.* In eastern Pennsylvania this mushroom is picked as widely as morels. Easy to identify and certainly easy to spot at the base of dying oaks and other hardwoods, it is a polypore that is always fleshy and firm, and the entire fungus is edible. In fact, I prefer the harder stems to the caps because of their resilient texture. The flavor is mild and goes well with smoked meats such as sausage and with cream sauces for pasta. This is a good candidate for pickling. *G. frondosa* is under study in AIDS research, having had similar effects as AZT without side effects. It also contains the polysaccharide beta 1.6 Glucan, also known as grifolan, which has been shown to be a potent antitumor substance in tests on laboratory mice.

Polyporus umbellatus Common name—umbrella polypore, *zhu ling, chorei-maitake, tsuchi-maitake,* Chinese sclerotium. Another significant fungus undergoing extensive research for its anticancer properties, this mushroom is treated and eaten in the same fashion as *G. frondosa.* It is fairly common in eastern Pennsylvania.

Laetiporus sulphureus Common name—sulphur shelf mushroom, chicken-of-the-woods. Growing on dead hardwoods and occasionally conifers, this is one of the most frustrating of the wild, edible, woody mushrooms. On the one hand, it's on everyone's list of easy-to-identify-you-can't-mistake-it mushrooms. On the other hand, your chances are less than fifty-fifty that you will be able to eat it. In a typical season in eastern Pennsylvania, only about twenty percent of the sulfurs we find are edible. Why? Because unless the mushroom is very young and very tender, it's a waste of time. When it is tender, it's an exceptional treat—spongy and melt-in-your-mouth delicious—and, yes, it does remind one of fresh succulent chicken breast. But if it grows in an arid environment, even if it's young, or if it gets too mature, which happens sooner than you think, forget it! I have carted home bushels of what I thought would be bright tender chicken mushroom dinners for weeks, only to boil them for hours and then chuck them into the garbage. (Some books tell you that the outer edges can be edible, and that is sometimes the case, but I've thrown away plenty of outer edges also.) Eating an unfit chicken mushroom is like trying to digest a piece of wood. It never softens and it leaves your mouth feeling dried out and exhausted. If after you have boiled this mushroom for fifteen minutes and it hasn't tenderized to your liking, just let it go and settle for store-bought. Good Luck!

Armillariella mellea   Common name—honey mushroom. Widely picked among the Polish population, this mushroom is very popular for canning and pickling mainly because you can't find just one. If they are out there, there are usually tons of them growing thickly on wood in huge clusters, as well as single specimens popping up out of the ground. You will notice that the cap is quite slimy when wet. That slime is somewhat muted after cooking and is not objectionable. Honey mushrooms are good for stews, but remember that the cap is tender but the stalk is too tough to eat and is best cut off while picking. Pickled honey mushrooms are great in salads and martinis. They are also good in cream sauces that have been enriched with sour cream or crème fraîche.

Fistulina hepatica   Common name—beefsteak mushroom, ox tongue. This mushroom elicits much argument among mycophiles; you either love it or hate it. It is one of the few mushrooms with a high vitamin C content, so it is more sour than most varieties. It is one of the few wild fungi that can be enjoyed raw in salads, and it can also be cooked—although it loses some of its sour flavor and takes on the character of—are you ready for this?—liver.

Auricularia Group   Common name—cloud ear, wood ear, tree ear, jelly fungus, *yung ngo, mu-er,* ear fungus, *kikurage, mokurage, aragekikurage.* This group consists of two species. *A. polytricha* and *A. auricula,* which are very close and are referred to interchangeably. They are the mushrooms found mostly dried in Asian grocery stores, and balloon up to great size when left to soak in warm water. In the past few years I have seen them fresh in the Chinatowns of New York and Philadelphia. Fresh or reconstituted, they are usually sliced thin because they remain very crunchy even after long cooking. They should be used in dishes where their crunchiness is a centerpiece of the experience, such as stir-fried dishes.

Hericium Group   Common name—tooth fungi, lion's mane, monkey's head, bear's head, old man's beard, Satyr's beard, pom pom, *pom pom blanc, yamabushi-take.* This group consists of *H. erinaceus, H. coralloides* (comb tooth), *H. abietis* (conifer coral hericium), *H. ramosum* (comb hericium), and *H. americanum.* Very much favored by mushroom lovers for their lobsterlike flavor when cooked, these mushrooms are usually sliced across the cascading "teeth" to give a lacelike appearance. They can then be prepared as other mushrooms are, but I like to drape them over fish and cook them *en papillote* with a few other vegetables.

Sparassis Group   Common name—cauliflower mushroom. There is always some disagreement among mycologists as to naming certain mushrooms, and this group is an example. However, as a genus it is quite unique and the names generally used for it are *S. crispa, S. radicata,* and *S. spathulata.* These mushrooms can grow to fifty pounds or more apiece and look as if someone found a perfectly even set of filelike sheets, then fanned them like a deck of cards, only in three dimensions. Anyway, they are considered choice, with a texture similar to jelly fungi but not quite as firm. They need to be cooked for at least an hour in chicken broth to become tender and then sliced for use. All this has to be done after you have cleaned them, which can be a real chore, as it is with a number of polypores. Still, it's fun to do with someone you love and a few glasses of wine. The nice thing about these mushrooms is that they stand up very well in stews that need long cooking.

Tomato Soup with Rosemary and Oyster Mushrooms

Use only fresh tomatoes in season, preferably from your own garden. Avoid the "trip-ripened" varieties from California or Florida.

Cut the tomatoes into quarters and place in a 6-quart saucepan. Add the beet, rosemary, salt, and sugar and bring to a boil. Reduce to a very light simmer and cover, stirring vigorously from time to time and mashing the tomatoes to extract the juice. Simmer for 1 hour.

While the soup is simmering, place the oil in a skillet over medium heat. Add the garlic and onion and sauté for 1 minute. Add the mushrooms and sauté for another minute.

Strain the tomato mixture through a fine sieve, and return the soup to the saucepan. Place over medium heat and return to a simmer. Add the mushrooms and stir. Serve in soup bowls garnished with a small sprig of rosemary.

Variation: French Tomato Soup. Proceed as above but garnish the soup with a large garlic crouton topped with a slice of fresh mozzarella. Place the crouton with the cheese in a low oven to soften the cheese and then carefully float atop the soup. Finally, sprinkle some finely chopped fresh basil over the cheese and serve.

Serves 4
Wine: Dry Creek Fume Blanc

---

2 pounds fresh ripe tomatoes

1/2 small red beet, shaved with a vegetable peeler into thin slivers

4 large sprigs fresh rosemary, plus additional for garnish

1/2 teaspoon salt

1/4 teaspoon sugar

1 tablespoon vegetable oil

1 garlic clove, finely chopped

1/2 small onion, chopped

4 ounces fresh oyster mushrooms, cleaned

Mexican Oyster Mushroom Soup

Tomatillos form the basis for one of Mexico's classic sauces, salsa verde. The green, citrusy fruit resembles a green tomato only in color, for its puckery acidic flavor is lemon more than anything else. There is an elegance and distinct character to the tomatillo that sets it apart. In this recipe, the edge is certainly there but it is muted to allow other flavors to come through.

You can use any exotic or wild mushroom for this soup.

Place the tomatillos, onion, garlic, 1 tablespoon of salt, the sugar, and chiles in a large saucepan. Add enough water just to cover and bring to a boil. Reduce the heat, cover, and let simmer for 15 minutes.

Place a large sauté pan over medium heat and add the chorizo. Break up the sausage into small bits. When the fat is rendered, about 5 minutes, add the mushrooms and sauté over low heat. The mushrooms will release a little liquid. Continue to sauté for 2 minutes, then season with a little salt. Set aside.

When the tomatillo mixture has simmered for 15 minutes, add the solid ingredients to a food processor and puree, adding the liquid from the pan as it purees until all the liquid is added. Strain the liquid through a sieve and back into the saucepan. It should be a pale green color and yield about 4 cups.

Add the mushrooms and chorizo to the liquid and simmer for another 5 minutes. Ladle into bowls, sprinkle the cilantro on top, and serve immediately.

Serves 4
Suggested wine: St. Francis Gewürztraminer

---

12 medium tomatillos, stems and husks removed

1 large onion, coarsely chopped

4 tablespoons chopped garlic

Salt

2 teaspoons sugar

2 serrano chiles or 1 jalapeño, coarsely chopped

6 ounces chorizo sausage

10 ounces fresh oyster mushrooms, cleaned

2 tablespoons chopped fresh cilantro

Tacos with Sulfur Shelf Mushrooms and Cactus

You can find cactus pads in Mexican grocery stores. Be careful of the little needles sticking out of the flesh. With gloves on, remove them with a potato peeler—and don't forget to get the ones on the edge.

Any firm fresh mushroom will work, and you won't have to boil them first the way you do with sulfur shelves. Just sauté the raw mushrooms with the cooked cactus.

Bring a large pot of lightly salted water to a boil. Add the cactus and sliced mushrooms. Simmer the mushrooms for 5 to 10 minutes, or until tender. Lift them out of the water and set aside. Continue to cook the cactus 15 to 20 minutes more. Drain on a plate lined with a paper towel.

Cut away the thicker bulbous portion at the base of the cactus pad and slice in pieces to approximate the size of the mushroom slices. The cactus will ooze a slightly viscous substance, as okra does.

Heat the oil in a large skillet and sauté the onion, red pepper, chiles, and garlic for 2 minutes. Add the cactus and mushrooms, and sauté for another 2 minutes. Salt to taste and fill each of the taco shells, allowing 2 tacos per person.

1 cactus pad, needles removed

12 ounces sulfur shelf mushrooms, cleaned and sliced

3 tablespoon vegetable oil

1 small onion, sliced

1 small red bell pepper, sliced

1 jalapeño or 2 serrano chiles, thinly sliced

1 teaspoon minced garlic

Salt

8 ready-to-eat taco shells

Serves 4
Suggested accompaniment: Mexican beer

Hen-of-the-Woods with Calamari and Chile Oil on Wet Sesame Rice

Any of the firmer fresh mushrooms can be used. This dish can also be prepared as a cold salad. Allow the mushrooms and calamari to chill, then toss with the peppers, some balsamic vinegar, and the chili oil and serve over mesclun.

In a saucepan, combine the rice, 1½ cups water, a little salt, the sesame oil, and the sesame seed. Bring to a boil, stir, reduce to a simmer, and cover with a tight-fitting lid. Cook until most of the moisture is absorbed, about 15 minutes. This rice will be wetter than what you may be used to.

Heat the olive and chile oils in a large sauté pan and sauté the pepper and scallions for 1 minute.

½ cup white rice

Salt

1 teaspoon roasted sesame oil

1 teaspoon toasted sesame seed (optional; available in Asian markets)

4 tablespoons olive oil

1 teaspoon chile oil (available in Asian markets)

1 large red bell pepper, seeded and thinly sliced

3 scallions, sliced down the middle, green part removed, and white cut into 2-inch pieces

12 ounces fresh hen-of-the-woods mushrooms, cleaned and cut into pieces 2 to 3 inches long along their natural lines

2 medium squid, cleaned and sliced

2 teaspoons soy sauce

1 teaspoon sugar

1 teaspoon cornstarch

Add the mushrooms and sauté for another 2 minutes. Add the squid and sauté until the squid just turns white, about 2 minutes. Combine the soy sauce, sugar, and cornstarch with ⅓ cup cold water in a small mixing bowl and stir well. Add this to the mushroom mixture and stir until thickened. Add a little water if the mixture gets too thick and adjust flavor with a little soy sauce. Remove from heat. Dish out the rice onto 4 plates, cover each mound with the mushrooms, and serve.

Serves 4
Suggested wine:
Girard Chenin Blanc

Grilled Rockfish with Stropharia, Fresh Tomatoes, and Balsamic Vinegar

This refreshing summertime dish can also be served over pasta. Any kind of delicate mushrooms such as Coprinus *can be substituted.*

Prepare a charcoal grill or preheat broiler.

Rub the fish with a little olive oil and salt.

Place the remaining oil and the vinegar in a large sauté pan over medium heat. Add the onion and sauté for 1 minute. Add the mushrooms and sauté until mushrooms begin to go

4 filets of fresh rockfish (striped bass), about 6 ounces each
5 tablespoons good olive oil
Salt
1 tablespoon balsamic vinegar
1 medium red onion, sliced
12 ounces fresh **Stropharia rugosa-annulata,** *cleaned and sliced*
2 large tomatoes, peeled, sliced, and seeded
1 teaspoon minced garlic
2 teaspoons chopped fresh dill
2 teaspoons chopped fresh basil
Grated Parmesan cheese

limp, about 2 minutes. Add the tomatoes, garlic, dill, and basil and sauté until most of the liquid has evaporated. Salt to taste and keep warm.

Grill the fish until done to your liking (do not overcook it!), place on plates, and cover with the tomato-mushroom mixture. Sprinkle some Parmesan cheese over the top of each filet and serve.

Serves 4
Suggested wine: Sauvignon Blanc

Deep-Fried Oyster Mushrooms Pressed with Walnuts and Chipotle

One of the most common ways to prepare button mushrooms is to bread them. This method also works well with less delicate varieties, such as larger oyster mushrooms. It helps both the flavor and texture to use nuts instead of bread crumbs, which add crunch to the dish. The dish can, of course, be made with button mushrooms or any wild mushrooms that are two to three inches wide across the cap. The frying will cook them sufficiently.

These mushrooms need no dipping sauce. If you prefer a milder flavor, use Chinese oyster sauce instead of the chipotle puree.

1 (7-ounce) can chipotle peppers
in adobo sauce
12 large fresh oyster mushrooms
1 quart oil, for frying
Flour
3 eggs, beaten
1/2 cup finely crushed walnuts

Place chipotle peppers in a blender with the liquid in the can and blend until smooth.

Clean the mushrooms leaving the stem on. Paint the mushrooms with the puree. Heat the oil in a deep saucepan to 340° F.

Using 3 small dishes, place some flour in one, the eggs in another, and in the remaining dish, the crushed walnuts. Coat the painted mushrooms with the flour, then dip into the eggs. Finally, coat the mushrooms with the walnuts and press the walnuts into the caps gently to ensure that they stay coated with the nuts.

Place several mushrooms in the hot oil. When the mushrooms are golden brown, in about 30 seconds, remove with a slotted spoon and place on a plate lined with a paper towel to drain. Let drain for 30 seconds and serve immediately.

Serves 4
Suggested wine: Ridge Petit Sirah

Beef Andy Warhol

The shock of cellophane noodles atop a pristine filet reminds me of Andy Warhol's hair. This dish was developed for a tasting of Opus 1 wines conducted by our friend, Dr. Halbert Ashworth, and his wife, Peggy.

Vietnamese whole grain soy sauce is thicker than the sauce you may be familiar with. Chinese oyster sauce is a good substitute. Both are available in most Asian markets, as are Chinese sausages.

Preheat the oven to 450° F.

Coat the filet with the Vietnamese soy sauce and let marinate at room temperature for 30 minutes. Place in oven and roast for 20 minutes for medium-rare.

While the filet is cooking, prepare the onions and mushrooms. Heat the butter in a skillet, add the sausage, and sauté for 2 minutes. Add the onions and sauté for 5 minutes more. Add ¼ cup water and the coriander, chili powder, garlic, lemon juice, black pepper, wine, salt, sugar, and soy sauce. Simmer for 10 minutes or until reduced to barely any liquid left.

Add the mushrooms, cover, and simmer over a low heat for 7 minutes. Remove the cover and stir. Keep on the heat until all residual liquid has evaporated, about 10 minutes. Remove from heat and keep warm.

Bring a pot of lightly salted water to a boil. Add the sesame oil and bring to a simmer. Add the noodles and turn off the heat. Let soak for 2 minutes, then drain. Keep warm.

Cut the meat into 4 equal pieces. Evenly divide the onion-mushroom mixture on 4 dinner plates. Top each with a piece of the filet, then spoon on some noodles. Serve immediately.

2 pound center-cut filet mignon

4 tablespoons Vietnamese soy sauce or Chinese oyster sauce

3 tablespoons butter

1 link Chinese sausage, thinly sliced

2 large red onions, thinly sliced

½ teaspoon ground coriander

½ teaspoon chili powder

1 teaspoon minced garlic

1 teaspoon lemon juice

¼ teaspoon black pepper

¼ cup dry red wine

1 teaspoon salt

1 teaspoon sugar

1 tablespoon soy sauce

5 ounces fresh oyster mushrooms, cleaned

1 tablespoon roasted sesame oil

3 ounces cellophane noodles

Serves 4

Suggested wine: Kenwood Cabernet Sauvignon or Bordeaux

Ziti with Chinese Sausage and Oyster Mushrooms

You may substitute any other kind of fresh mushrooms. If you like spicy dishes, add some sliced jalapeños when you add the scallions.

Bring a large pot of lightly salted water to a boil. Add the ziti, stir, and cover, reduce to a simmer, and cook until al dente, about 10 minutes.

While the ziti is cooking, heat the peanut oil in a large sauté pan or wok. Add the sausage and sauté until some of the fat in the sausage begins to blend with the peanut oil, about 3 minutes. Add the

> 4 ounces ziti
>
> 3 tablespoons peanut or vegetable oil
>
> 2 links Chinese sausage, thinly sliced (available in Asian markets)
>
> 1 teaspoon roasted sesame oil
>
> 1 bunch scallions, white part and 1 inch into the dark green sliced into 1-inch pieces
>
> ½ pound fresh oyster mushrooms, cleaned and sliced
>
> 3 tablespoons Chinese oyster sauce

Serves 4
Suggested wine: Heitz Grignolino

sesame oil, then add the scallions and sauté for 30 seconds. Stir in the mushrooms and sauté for 2 minutes, until the mushrooms go limp. Add the oyster sauce and stir to combine. Remove from the heat.

Drain the ziti in a colander, pour into a bowl, add the mushroom mixture, and mix. Serve immediately.

Phoenix Fritters

Yet another name for our multifaceted Pleurotus is phoenix. These fritters make a nice hors d'oeuvre because they aren't messy to eat. They can be enjoyed alone or with an accompanying sauce, such as a mustard mayonnaise.

> 1 quart corn oil, for frying
>
> 18 large whole oyster mushrooms
>
> 1 egg
>
> ⅓ cup half-and-half
>
> ½ teaspoon salt
>
> 1 teaspoon soy sauce
>
> ½ cup all-purpose flour
>
> Dash of cayenne pepper

Heat the corn oil in a 4-quart saucepan to 400° F.

Clean the mushrooms of dirt.

Combine the egg, half-and-half, salt, soy sauce, flour, and cayenne pepper and whip with a whisk until smooth.

In small batches, submerge the mushrooms in the batter but keep them separated. Place mushrooms in the hot oil 2 to 3 at a time, keeping them well separated, and fry until golden brown, about 30 seconds. Remove from oil and set on a paper towel to drain. Serve immediately.

Serves 4
Suggested wine: Guenoc Meritage White

Honey Mushrooms with Savory, Thyme, and Chicken

Long a favorite of wild mushroom hunters, the honey mushroom is as versatile as it is delicious. This recipe can be enjoyed in a ragout or casserole with leftover chicken or turkey. Other mushrooms can be used, but they should be soft, pliant varieties like shiitake rather than buttons or portobellos.

Heat the butter in a large sauté pan over medium heat. Add the onion and sauté for 1 minute. Add the mushrooms and continue to sauté until the mushrooms sweat and release their liquid into the pan, about 5 minutes. Add the sour cream or crème fraîche and stir to blend with the mushrooms. Add the thyme, savory, and sugar, and season to taste with salt and pepper.

Mix in the chicken, and let the mixture simmer until it thickens, about 2 minutes. Stir in the parsley, spoon mixture into the kataifi nests, and serve.

Serves 4
Suggested wine: Pinot Blanc

4 tablespoons butter
1 medium onion, chopped
1 pound fresh honey mushrooms, caps only, cleaned
¾ cup sour cream or crème fraîche
1 teaspoon dried thyme
1 teaspoon dried savory
¼ teaspoon sugar
Salt and pepper
1½ cups leftover cooked chicken, off the bone
2 tablespoons finely chopped fresh parsley
4 kataifi nests (see page 64)

Spinach with Cloud Ears, Basil, and Pine Nuts

You can hardly see the cloud ears in the dish, but along with the pine nuts, they add a firmness to the spinach, making it fun to chew. This dish is a great accompaniment to lamb, but can also be a vegetarian entree for two, and makes a tasty stuffing (with a little goat cheese) for ravioli.

Cloud ears (Auricularia polytricha) *now come in small (.88-ounce) packages from Franklin Farms, already thinly sliced and ready to use in this recipe. If you use the whole cloud ears that are often found in Asian grocery stores, you must soak them in hot water until they are crunchy but not hard. You can even simmer the mushrooms gently to hasten this process. Then cool the cloud ears, slice them thinly, and proceed with the rest of the recipe, using 1 instead of 2 cups water described below.*

2 tablespoons extra-virgin olive oil

1/3 cup thinly sliced white part of scallions or onion

2 tablespoons pine nuts, toasted

1 (.88-ounce) package thinly sliced and dried cloud ears

1 packed cup coarsely chopped fresh basil or 1 tablespoon dried

1/2 teaspoon salt

10 ounces fresh spinach

Pour the olive oil into a large saucepan over medium heat. Add the scallions or onion and sauté until they begin to soften, about 2 minutes. Add the pine nuts and stir for 2 minutes.

Add the cloud ears, basil, salt, and 2 cups water. Bring to a boil and cook for about 10 minutes to reconstitute the mushrooms.

Add the spinach, turn up the heat, and stir until spinach is wilted. Turn the heat down and simmer the mixture until most of the water has evaporated, stirring occasionally, about 5 minutes. Correct for salt if necessary and serve.

Serves 4 as a side dish, 2 as an entree
Suggested wine: A grassy Sauvignon Blanc (when served as an entree)

Westphalian Sovereign Mushrooms

Among my first encounters with cultivated oyster mushrooms were those being produced by the Campbell Soup Company here in Reading, Pennsylvania. Wishing to avoid confusion with other brands by simply calling them by their recognized common name, Campbell decided to trademark their Pleurotus by giving it the name Sovereign. Since Westphalian ham is used in this recipe the name became Westphalian Sovereigns. Ah! What's-in-a-name? As it turned out, this recipe became a regular in the restaurant because of its popularity.

This method of preparing mushrooms is universally excellent for any kind of fresh mushroom, but is generally recommended for those varieties that have less assertive flavors.

---

2 tablespoons vegetable oil

½ small onion, thinly sliced

1 teaspoon minced garlic

½ pound fresh medium oyster mushrooms (sliced in half if larger), cleaned

½ ounce Westphalian ham or prosciutto, finely chopped

1 cup heavy cream

1 teaspoon soy sauce

½ tablespoon cream sherry

½ tablespoon chopped fresh parsley

½ tablespoon cornstarch mixed with ¼ cup water

Salt

4 puff pastry shells (available in freezer section of most supermarkets)

In a large skillet, heat the oil over medium heat. Add the onion and garlic and sauté until the onion becomes translucent, about 3 minutes.

Add the mushrooms, keeping the heat on medium, and sauté, stirring occasionally, for 3 minutes. The mushrooms will begin to give off liquid, but some of this will evaporate as the mushrooms cook. Do not allow the mushrooms to cook so rapidly that all the liquid evaporates, because you want to keep some of this flavorful essence. Once the mushroom liquid just covers the mushrooms, add the ham and cook for 10 minutes over low heat.

Stir in the cream, soy sauce, and sherry and return to a light simmer, then reduce heat and simmer for 6 minutes.

Stir the parsley into the mushrooms, then add some of the cornstarch mixture a little bit at a time until the mushroom sauce has thickened. You may not have to use all of the cornstarch. Add salt to taste.

Spoon immediately into pastry shells and serve.

Serves 4
Suggested wine: rich, woody Chardonnay

Shiitake

FROM THE EAST

Asian Mushrooms

THERE IS NO BOOK IN THE ENGLISH language that describes the plethora of mushrooms either raised or picked wild in Asia. What little we know of mushroom cultivation in the West has been standard practice there for many years, and we are just beginning to appreciate the contributions that Asia has made in growing and researching mushrooms.

One thing we do know for certain. The Asian perception of mushrooms is fundamentally different from our own. In the West, we tend to view mushrooms as a culinary embellishment, or as just another vegetable. We know that they taste intriguing and readily accept mushrooms on our plate, but we do so as an exception to our daily habits. The Chinese and Japanese, on the other hand, view mushrooms as a health food, as indispensable to good health as we consider salad greens to be. How and when this came about is not known, but it is certain that the consumption of mushrooms is carefully woven into the cultures and diets of many Asian households and that the medicinal benefits of mushrooms are common knowledge. Mushroom cultivation is even associated with the production of other foods. For example, soybean roughage *(okara),* the main by-product of making tofu and tempeh, can be manipulated and enriched to be a substrate for the production of some species of oyster mushrooms *(Pleurotus),* reishi *(Ganoderma lucidum),* and even morels.

Mushrooms: The Ultimate Health Food

Most scientific literature on the curative powers of mushrooms comes from Japan and China, but these studies have been so startling that serious work is now being initiated in the United States. What was once considered to be in the realm of "folk medicine" has received some substantiation in research from Japan and China, which is now being seriously studied throughout the world.

Much of the work in Asia centers on the medicinal use of mushrooms for treatment of cancer. Laboratory mice with tumors have been successfully treated with various mushrooms or extracts from mushrooms, including species from the genera *Coprinus, Flammulina, Lentinus, Polyporus, Hericium,* and *Auricularia.* And though most of this work has been with laboratory animals, not all of it has. U.S. researchers visiting Beijing in 1983 were told that a tea made from *Polyporus umbellatus* was given to lung cancer patients after radiation therapy. Most of these patients experienced complete recovery in a few years, whereas the majority of the control group had died. In addition, the tea treatment dramatically improved the quality of life of the affected patients, characterized by increased appetites and the absence of malaise. An epidemiological study in Japan found that a community of enoki growers near the city of Nagano had unusually low rates of cancer. Frequent enoki consumption was thought to be the cause. Further, Chinese physicians reportedly are using extracts of *zhu ling (P. umbellatus)* in the treatment of lung cancer, cancer of the esophagus, stomach cancer, liver cancer, intestinal cancer, leukemia, breast cancer, and lymphosarcoma. In the United States, the National Cancer Institute is testing sclerotia (a dormant phase of mushroom growth) of this mushroom in its AIDS and cancer programs, in part owing to the efforts of mushroom experts Paul Stamets and Dr. Andrew Weil.

Research done by the National Cancer Institute through its Anti-HIV Drug Testing System, under the Developmental Therapeutics Program, has already shown that the AIDS virus is vulnerable to extracts from fruiting bodies of *Grifola frondosa.* This is the first mushroom with anti-HIV activity to be confirmed by researchers in both Japan and the United States. In fact, it compares favorably with the much better known AZT, but without the latter's negative side effects. In China, polypores are generally considered effective in shoring up the immune system.

Every year researchers isolate at least ten additional antibiotics from mushrooms. This is because mushrooms must compete against bacteria, and they are equipped with biological weapons to survive in that environment. This is perhaps the best reason for adding not one but many varieties of mushrooms to your diet. You may be effectively arming yourself against infections in the most natural way possible. Penicillin was derived, after all, from a fungus.

There are other areas in which mushrooms have been found to be effective against disease. Oyster mushrooms have been used to treat pulmonary emphysema in China, and *Auricularia polytricha* was discovered to have a potent anticoagulant property. Japanese studies with *shiitake* have shown them to be effective in reducing cholesterol levels in the blood.

What is truly interesting is that all of this research has been done on a limited number of mushrooms, and the work is just beginning in the West. What the Chinese and Japanese have known for centuries is now being discovered here: mushrooms are the ultimate health food.

Varieties of Asian Mushrooms

Lentinus edodes Common name—shiitake, golden oak mushroom, black forest mushroom, black mushroom, oakwood mushroom, oak tree mushroom, Chinese mushroom, *shiangu-gu, donku, pasania.* Grown in Japan for more than a thousand years, shiitake are considered to be the finest eating mushroom in Asia. They derive their name from the shii tree, on which they grow wild in Japan. They also grow on dead or dying Asian oaks and beeches, but have never been found wild in North America. The first written record on the subject of growing shiitake comes from Wu

Sang Kwuang, who was born during the Sung Dynasty (960–1127 A.D.). The origin of cultivation may be much earlier. The standard method was to inoculate logs with cultured mycelium. After six months to a year, the logs would bear mushrooms. Modern methods of cultivation, such as using sawdust instead of logs and bringing the whole operation indoors, have cut that time to several weeks.

The most wonderful aspect of shiitake is their flavor. Distinct and slightly smoky, they adapt very well to stronger flavors in a dish. Other mushrooms roll over and die whenever a spice is added to a casserole, but shiitake take it on, absorbing it and wearing it like an ornament. This attribute, in addition to its inherent flavor, make it one of the most revered mushrooms in Asian cooking. There is even a Japanese wine called Healthy Wine, which is made from shiitake. Shiitake have been cultivated for so long in Asia that many strains exist, which is why there is such wide variation in size and general meatiness of the mushrooms. It is one of the few mushrooms of any sort that are regularly enjoyed raw as well as cooked, although I still prefer them cooked because their flavor changes dramatically. Lentinan, an extract from shiitake, is known throughout Asia as a potent anticancer drug. It has also been shown that shiitake have been very effective in reducing blood cholesterol when eaten regularly.

The production of fresh shiitake has boomed in this country in the last ten years, to the point where they are commonplace in supermarket produce sections. Just pick nice, firm caps that have a spongy feel rather than limp, older ones. The stems of shiitake are fibrous and can only be eaten when small and immature. Dried shiitake have always been available in Asian grocery stores and are becoming less popular because the fresh are so widely available. However, it is a good idea to keep a supply of dried ones on hand because they yield a rich liquid when reconstituted and remain one of the few dried mushrooms that reconstitute into a good substitute for fresh mushrooms.

Pholiota nameko   Common name—nameko, slime pholiota, viscid mushroom. Nameko are very popular in Japan, second only to shiitake in volume raised each year. They have a surprisingly pleasant flavor, but their one drawback is a very viscid (okay, slimy) cap, which may be why they have not been widely cultivated in this country. However, the slime disappears with cooking. The Chinese have shown that extracts of this mushroom increase resistance to Staphylococcus bacteria. They are available canned in some stores and are good in stir-fried dishes and, especially, in soups.

Flammulina velutipes   Common name—enoki, *enokitake (enokidake),* winter mushroom, velvet foot, furry foot, golden mushroom, *nametake, yuki-motase.* The Japanese call this the "Snow Peak Mushroom," and in the wild it has a brightly colored yellow to orange cap. The cultivated version looks, however, like cultivated white hair pins, with none of the color and a greatly reduced cap. I find it best to use enoki raw in salads or added at the last moment to soups for some visual intrigue. Some claim to really enjoy the flavor, which I find mild and pleasant but not distinct.

Agrocybe aegerita   Common name—black poplar mushroom, swordbelt agrocybe, *yanagi-matsutake, zhuzhhaung-tiantougu.* Generally wild but capable of cultivation, this is an excellent candidate for stump recycling in the southeastern United States, according to mushroom expert Paul Stamets. It is widely consumed in Japan and China and has also been cultivated in Europe, where it is considered a delicacy.

Hypholoma sublateritium   Common name—*kuritake,* brick top, red woodlover. Cultivated in Japan but not yet in the United States, the *kuritake* is a good all-around mushroom that is quite commonly picked wild in this country, in great batches off of dead hardwood trees.

The *Shimeji* Group   *Shimeji* is a widely used word for several types of delicious mushrooms grown and consumed in Japan. The true *shimeji,* which the Japanese refer to as *hon-shimeji,* is really *Lyophyllum shimeji,* which ironically is not a cultivated type. The cultivated species, which is often referred to as *buna-shimeji,* is really a look-alike, *Hypsizygus tessulatus,* or the beech mushroom. Other names are *yamabiko hon-shimeji* and *tamo-motashi.* The Japanese have reduced their cultivation of oyster mushrooms in favor of this one because of its superior texture, which is firm and crunchy, and its flavor, which is sweetly nutty. This will perhaps be the next big "boom" cultivatable exotic mushroom in this country. Another species, *Hypsizygus ulmarius* (the elm oyster mushroom, *shirotamogitake*) is also popular in Japan. It more closely resembles the oyster mushroom as we know it, with similar texture and flavor. It also has potential for commercialization in this country because it can, like the portobello, grow quite large. Use both for stir-fried dishes.

Volvariella volvace   Common name—paddy straw mushroom, straw mushroom, Chinese mushroom, *fukurotake.* More widely cultivated than most other mushrooms in Asia, the paddy straw mushroom is economically critical to the farmers of Thailand, Cambodia, Vietnam, and Taiwan as well as China. Those who have tasted the fresh ones claim that the canned variety (which are common in Asian grocery stores in this country) are vastly inferior. However, that is all that is available at present, and that will probably continue to be the case since this mushroom can be grown only in very warm climates. The mushrooms come canned in peeled and unpeeled (egglike) forms. They are good in stir-fry dishes and for pickling. We pickle them and use them in Martinis at Joe's.

Ganoderma lucidum   Common name—*reishi, ling chi, ling zhi, mannentake, saiwai-take, sarunouchi-take,* panacea polypore. No discussion of Asian mushrooms, particularly in conjunction with their health properties, can be termed complete without mentioning *reishi.* I first became aware of this mushroom when some friends who own a local mushroom farm brought me a few specimens. They had recently been to China, where they had received these as a gift, but they did not know anything about them. Neither did I, but a few weeks later we were fortunate to have as a guest at our restaurant the former associate minister of agriculture of the People's Republic of China. He explained that *ling chi* was not a gourmet's mushroom, but was more like ginseng in being a potent medicine. This made sense because the *ling zhi* is a very hard, shiny polypore that softens only after many hours in water or wine, which is then ingested. Or, one can break the mushroom into small pieces with a hammer then grind it into powder for sprinkling on other foods. It is deeply revered throughout Asia, where it is credited with helping its users achieve long life, sexual prowess (*ling zhi* is traditionally given to men by women to express sexual interest), health, and general well-being. According to Paul Stamets, "*reishi* has become the natural medicine of choice by North Americans, and has become especially popular amongst high-risk, HIV-infected groups in recent years." A complex group of polysaccharides have been isolated that stimulate the immune system. Reports also have confirmed its role as an anticoagulant and its ability to lower cholesterol levels. Studies on mice at the Texas Health Science Center in San Antonio showed that it has anti-inflammatory properties comparable to hydrocortisone. It is also used in the treatment of arthritis.

Armillaria matsutake, Armillaria ponderosa, Armillaria caligata   Common name—white matsutake. In stingy seasons this mushroom can command prices in Japan comparable to fresh Italian or French truffles. I have bought them for less than twenty dollars a pound in normal seasons. One of the reasons matsutake can get so expensive is that it is subject to the whims of Mother Nature. Even though Japan leads the world in types of successfully cultivated mushrooms, the beloved matsutake can be found only in the wild. Although some claim the mushroom is tough, I have not found this to be the case, although I know there are some years when certain varieties are definitely firmer and require longer cooking. I also suspect that this is part of the appeal of matsutake to the Japanese, who prefer food that sometimes bites back. The flavor and scent have a mild, appealing resinlike character not unlike the *Tricholoma* we pick here in the fall. The Japanese *A. matsutake* is probably closer to a similar mushroom picked on the West Coast, *A. caligata,* which can be fragrant—sometimes fragrant to the point of being noisome. The mushroom usually sent to Japan from the United States is the *A. ponderosa,* or white matsutake. It is enjoyed here as well by Asian Americans and has a character that is distinct. Use it in stir-fries and soups.

Sautéed Nameko with Angel Hair Pancakes and Five-Spice Powder

Use this recipe as an appetizer for a dinner featuring fish as a main course.

Place the pasta in a large pot of boiling salted water. Cook for about 3 minutes after the water comes back to a boil, then drain.

Beat the eggs and add the cream and basil. Blend this well with the drained pasta and check for salt, adjusting if necessary.

Place about 2 tablespoons of the oil in a large sauté pan and heat until the oil causes a drop of water to "dance" on the surface before evaporating. This means the pan is ready for frying the pancakes. With tongs, pull out a quantity of the pasta equal to about a quarter of the total. Fry in the pan on both sides until the pancake is golden brown, about 45 seconds on each side. Repeat until all the pasta is used, adding more oil as needed. Keep warm.

Place 2 tablespoons of the oil in another large sauté pan over medium heat. Add the scallions and sauté for 1 minute. Add the mushrooms and sauté until they become somewhat limp and begin to give off liquid, about 3 minutes. Add 1 teaspoon salt, the sugar, soy sauce, and five-spice powder. Blend well. If necessary, add the cornstarch mixture and stir until thickened. It should not be runny.

Place a pancake in the middle of each plate and cover with the mushrooms and serve.

8 ounces angel hair pasta
2 eggs
2 tablespoons heavy cream
1 teaspoon dried basil
Salt
Vegetable oil
1 bunch scallions, sliced into 1-inch-long pieces on the bias
12 ounces fresh nameko
1 teaspoon sugar
1 tablespoon soy sauce
2 teaspoons Chinese five-spice powder (available at Asian markets)
1 tablespoon cornstarch mixed with 1/4 cup water

Serves 4
Suggested wine: St. Francis Gewürztraminer

Pakistani-Style Mushrooms in Pita

During my brief period at Cornell University twenty-five years ago, I became good friends with a Pakistani student. He often pined for the food of his homeland, and on many occasions we stopped at the grocery store on the way to his apartment and gathered the ingredients for a Pakistani-style supper.

This is Middle Eastern comfort food at its best. No forks are allowed, even if your beer bottle becomes too slippery to hold.

Heat the oil in a large skillet over medium heat until it begins

4 tablespoons vegetable oil

4 crushed garlic cloves, chopped

2 teaspoons ground cardamom

2 teaspoons ground cumin

4 dried hot chiles, crushed, or 4 jalapeño chiles, sliced

2 large onions, sliced

2 large tomatoes, sliced

1 small eggplant, peeled and thinly sliced, then cut crosswise to julienne

15 to 20 fresh shiitake caps, stems removed and caps sliced in half

Salt

Pita breads, lightly heated, or lightly toasted white bread

to smoke. Add the garlic, cardamom, cumin, and chiles. Stir vigorously for half a minute, then add the onions, tomatoes, eggplant, and shiitake. Stir over high heat, adding more oil if necessary. Sauté until the vegetables are well cooked, limp, and fragrant, about 10 minutes. Salt to taste. Stuff the pitas with the mixture and serve. Remember, no forks except to fill the pita pockets.

Makes 1 cup cooked filling
Suggested accompaniment: beer

Squid with Shiitake

When you spy fresh squid in the market, grab it. Buy it cleaned if you can, but if you can't it's always fun to do it yourself at home, squirting anyone within reach with the ink if you've got good aim or, more likely, making a mess if you don't. In any case, it's something that can only be described as a culinary bonding ritual. This is best served with sticky rice or noodles.

Cut the squid into bite-size pieces, cutting the body into thick rings, and lightly salt.

In a large sauté pan (or a wok if you have one), begin heating

1½ pounds cleaned squid
Salt
2 tablespoons vegetable oil
2 tablespoons peanut oil
1 bunch scallions, white parts only, cut on the diagonal into 1-inch pieces
1 tablespoon finely chopped fresh ginger
1 tablespoon chopped garlic
1 link Chinese sausage (available at Asian markets)
2 serrano chiles or 1 jalapeño, finely chopped (optional)
8 ounces fresh shiitake, stems removed (if shiitake are large, cut them in half)
1 tablespoon hoisin sauce
1 tablespoon Chinese oyster sauce
Cooked rice or noodles

the oils. Just as the oil barely begins to smoke, add the scallions, ginger, garlic, sausage, and chiles. Stir-fry for 1 minute. Add the mushrooms and stir-fry for another minute. Finally, add the squid and stir-fry until the squid becomes pearly white in color, about 1½ minutes, keeping the heat fairly high while you are stir-frying.

Add the hoisin and oyster sauces and blend well for 30 seconds. Serve over rice or noodles.

Serves 4
Suggested wine: Caymus Conundrum

Shiitake Japanese Style

Dipping and simmering sauces are favorites of the Japanese chef. The magical interplay of ingredients such as mirin, sake, and good soy sauce help define the flavor of Japanese cuisine. Mushrooms treated in this manner tend to lose some of their natural flavor, so be sure to use a mushroom that is assertive. The shiitake is ideal.

You will find that this is a very versatile way to prepare mushrooms. They go well with grilled meats, either as an accompaniment or right on the skewer with lamb or beef. They can be chilled and sliced and added to salads, or tossed warm into a salad with walnut oil and sage vinegar.

The marinade, once used, can be chilled and used again several times. Remember that each time, however, it will become more diluted by the liquid from the mushrooms.

> *20 fresh shiitake caps*
> *²⁄₃ cup good-quality sake*
> *4 tablespoons dark soy sauce*
> *2¹⁄₂ tablespoons mirin*
> *2¹⁄₂ tablespoons sugar*

Clean the mushroom caps and remove stems.

In a saucepan, combine the sake, soy sauce, mirin, and sugar and bring to a boil. Reduce to a simmer and add the mushrooms. Simmer for 7 minutes. Remove mushrooms and use in a salad immediately, or cool and use later with grilled meats.

Serves 4 as side dish or in salad

Enoki Salad with Cèpe Oil and Watercress-Savory Puree

Try this for a refreshing spring salad.

Reserve a few of the watercress and savory leaves for a garnish. Trim the stems of the remainder and place in a blender with 2 tablespoons water and the vinegar. Process until you have a fine puree. Set aside.

> *¹⁄₂ cup packed fresh watercress*
> *¹⁄₂ cup packed fresh savory*
> *1¹⁄₂ teaspoon white wine vinegar*
> *3 ounces enoki mushrooms, stems trimmed*
> *4 asparagus spears, cut into fine julienne*
> *Salt*
> *2 teaspoons lemon juice*
> *¹⁄₃ cup Cèpe Oil (page 89)*

Toss the enoki with the sliced asparagus, salt to taste, and lemon juice. Divide the salad among 4 plates. Pour the oil around the salad, then drizzle some of the watercress-savory puree over the oil in a decorative fashion. Serve, garnished with the watercress and savory leaves.

Serves 4

Fiddlehead Fern Salad with Enoki

I met Georges Blanc on a trip to France several years ago. I first noticed him sitting in the dining room at Restaurant Troigros and kept nudging Heidi and pointing like a good American tourist. No, of course it couldn't be, she said. That's funny I thought, it sure looks like the guy in the pictures from The Natural Cuisine of Georges Blanc, *which Heidi had bought for me a few months before. Later, I noticed one of the Troigros nephews conversing with the gentleman in question in the lobby. When the nephew saw me, he came over to introduce me to, yes, Georges Blanc. His book was a revelation to me. Suffice it to say, it had a profound influence on me. We dined at his restaurant several days later. The grace and artistry of the man are everywhere in his restaurant and small hotel, but especially on his plates. The fiddlehead fern salad described here was inspired by a leek dish in his book.*

Fiddlehead ferns (the beginning stage of certain edible ferns) are available from early April to the end of June from various parts of the country. Some people pick their own, but you must be careful, because several varieties of ferns are toxic. Only buy them from a reliable commercial source. Early fiddleheads tend to be somewhat bitter and do not lose that characteristic on cooking. The later fiddleheads are sweeter tasting with a slight anise character. The ends tend to dry and blacken, so just snip these off.

> **THE FIDDLEHEADS**
> ½ cup vegetable oil
> ½ cup white wine vinegar
> 2 teaspoons salt
> 2 teaspoons sugar
> Generous mixture of fresh herbs, such as savory, rosemary, thyme
> ½ cup finely chopped onion
> 2 teaspoons minced garlic
> 64 fiddlehead ferns (about ½ pound)
>
> **THE SAUCE**
> 1 (8-ounce) can beets, with liquid
> 1 tablespoon onion powder
> 1 tablespoon red wine vinegar
> 1 serrano chile, seeded and finely chopped
> Salt
>
> **THE GARNISH**
> ½ cup enoki
> 8 small sprigs lovage or parsley

Two days ahead, combine the vegetable oil, vinegar, salt, sugar, herbs, onion, and garlic, and whisk vigorously. Set aside. The marinade is best left for a day or two while it absorbs the flavor of the herbs.

Wash the fiddleheads thoroughly and snip off any black ends. Place ferns in a saucepan that will fit them and add about ½ inch water to the pan. Heat over medium heat until water begins to boil, then cover with a tight-fitting lid and steam the fiddleheads until they are tender but still crunchy, about 15 minutes.

(continued on page 160)

Fiddlehead Fern Salad with Enoki

(continued from page 159)

Remove from heat and plunge ferns into ice water to stop cooking. Remove from water after 5 minutes and set aside.

Strain the marinade to remove the herb pieces. Pour it over the ferns, cover, and refrigerate overnight.

Process the beets, onion powder, red wine vinegar, and chile in a blender until completely smooth. This sauce should be somewhat thick but easy to dispense from a mustard or ketchup squeeze container with a fairly thin spout head. Place the sauce in the container and refrigerate.

Remove the ferns from the marinade and drain on paper towels. Arrange on a plate in the form of a grape cluster, beginning with 5 at the top, then 4 in the next row in the spaces from the top row, then 3 in the next row in the spaces from the previous row, finishing with a single large fern at the bottom. There should be 15 fiddleheads per plate, with an additional one pulled out to simulate a stem in the middle of the top row.

From the plastic ketchup container, dispense the beet sauce around the bottom half of the fern cluster. Sprinkle with the enoki, and arrange the lovage sprigs at the base of the "stem" and the top of the first row to simulate leaves. Serve immediately because the sauce will bleed a thin liquid if left to stand.

Serves 4

Barbecued Oysters with Shiitake

You really can't get much simpler or more delicious than this dish. Either use this recipe or your own favorite barbecue sauce for the oysters.

You can also use caps of domestic button mushrooms, but make sure they are large enough, and you will probably have to add 2 minutes to the baking time.

---

1 tablespoon Chinese oyster sauce

1 tablespoon hoisin sauce

2 teaspoons ketchup

½ serrano chile, seeded and finely chopped

12 medium to large fresh shiitake caps

Olive oil

12 fairly large oysters, shucked

Preheat the oven to 325° F. Combine the oyster sauce, hoisin sauce, ketchup, and serrano chile and mix well. Let sit for several minutes to let the serrano flavor the rest of the sauce. This step can be done well ahead. Make sure the stems are completely cut off the mushroom caps. Paint the caps with a little oil and just a little of the barbecue sauce. Place the caps on a baking sheet and bake for 2 minutes.

While the caps are baking, roll the oysters in the rest of the barbecue sauce so that they are evenly coated. Remove the caps from the oven and place an oyster on each cap. Return to the oven for 5 minutes. Remove and place on serving dishes and serve immediately.

Serves 4
Suggested wine: Zinfandel

Pickled Straw Mushrooms

Although more decorative than rich in earthy mushroom flavor, pickled mushrooms nevertheless have their place. They are useful adjuncts to salads and great for plopping into a martini. The key is the proper balance of sugar to vinegar and the choice of herbs and seasonings. One thing to remember, however, is that strong acid mixtures like marinades or pickling solutions completely mask mushroom flavor and are therefore best used with mild-tasting mushroom varieties. I like to use canned Chinese straw mushrooms, but any variety will do. If you are pickling fresh mushrooms, you must blanch them first, because otherwise the liquid drawn from the mushrooms will dilute the solution and throw off its balance.

> *½ cup white wine vinegar*
> *¼ cup sugar*
> *1 tablespoon kosher (coarse) salt*
> *1 tablespoon dried pickling spices (or any combination of fresh or dried herbs) or ½ cup packed fresh herbs, such as savory, thyme, oregano, or basil*
> *3 (15-ounce) cans Chinese peeled straw mushrooms, or 20 ounces blanched fresh mushrooms*

In a medium saucepan, combine the vinegar, sugar, and salt with 1½ cups of water. Bring to a boil, stirring to dissolve the sugar and salt, and simmer for 5 minutes. Add the spices or herbs and steep, off the heat, for a few minutes.

Add the mushrooms and return to a simmer for 30 minutes. Let cool and cover. These will keep for weeks in the refrigerator.

Makes 4 cups

Breads Stuffed with Shiitake and Ham

This is great with a mushroom omelet (page 107) for Sunday lunch.

Cover the dried shiitake with water and bring to a boil. Simmer for 20 minutes, then remove from heat and cool. When cooled, slice thinly.

Heat the oil in a large sauté pan. Add the fresh or reconstituted shiitake, the ham, and the garlic. Sauté for 5 minutes, then let cool.

Place the flour in a large bowl of a mixer fitted with a dough hook. Combine 3 cups water, the salt, and sugar and heat to about 110° F. Remove from the heat. Stir to dissolve the sugar and salt. Stir in the yeast and let proof for 10 minutes; that is, the mixture should begin to foam from the activity of the yeast. If there is no foaming after 10 minutes, use another batch of yeast and repeat the process.

Add the yeast mixture gradually to the flour while mixing with the dough hook. Incorporate all of the liquid, then add the olive oil and herbs and blend until the dough comes cleanly away from the bowl. You may have to add some flour if the dough is too sticky. When the dough is ready, lay it out on a clean surface and knead for 1 minute. Place in a large greased bowl, cover, and let rise until doubled in bulk, about 1 hour in a draft-free spot.

Punch down the dough, then cut either in half or in fourths, depending on the size loaves you want. Roll out a piece of the dough with a rolling pin so that it is about ½ inch thick. Spread some of the cooled mushroom mixture evenly over the dough, then roll up the dough, tucking in the sides. Repeat for each piece of dough.

Place each rolled and stuffed piece on a lined baking sheet, cover lightly, and let rise in a warm place until tripled, about 2 hours.

Preheat the oven to 325° F.

Bake loaves for 35 to 45 minutes. Remove and let stand 15 minutes before slicing. This bread can be frozen for up to 4 weeks.

Makes 2 large or 4 smaller loaves

---

1 ounce dried shiitake or 20 to 30 fresh shiitake caps, thinly sliced

3 tablespoons vegetable oil

8 ounces Virginia ham, diced

1 tablespoon minced garlic

6 cups bread flour

1 tablespoon salt

1 tablespoon sugar

2 tablespoons active dry yeast

¼ cup olive oil

2 tablespoons finely chopped fresh savory and thyme or 2 teaspoons dried

Matsutake in Dashi

Dashi is indispensable in Japanese cooking—the equivalent of chicken stock in much of traditional European cookery. It is a fish-based stock with the addition of dried konbu (kelp) and dried bonito flakes, which is one of those seemingly inscrutable items you stare at on the shelf of an Asian grocery store. There is an intense charm about dashi.

Fresh shiitake can be substituted for the matsutake. Konbu is available in health food stores in 1.76 ounce packages. Just use the whole package. Dried, flaked bonito is available in several-sized packages.

1½ ounces dried konbu (kelp)
¾ ounce dried flaked bonito
8 ounces fresh matsutake, cleaned and cut into ¼-inch-wide slices, both stem and cap
2 teaspoons salt
1 tablespoon tamari or soy sauce
2 whole scallions, thinly sliced

Place 2 quarts of water in a large pot and put over medium heat. Rub the konbu pieces with a damp cloth and place in the pot. Bring to a very gentle simmer and keep it at that level without boiling for 15 minutes. It is important that the water not become too hot, as the flavor of the konbu is very delicate.

After 15 minutes, add the bonito flakes and simmer for another 10 minutes. Turn off the heat and allow to stand for 30 minutes.

Strain the liquid through a fine sieve into another saucepan. Add the mushrooms, salt, and soy sauce, and simmer for 20 minutes. Remove from the heat, pour into 4 bowls, divide the scallions equally among them, and serve.

Serves 4
Suggested accompaniment: Sake

Belgian Endive Salad with Mushrooms

I never make this salad the same way twice. Although the same marinade and pickled ginger should always be used, there are endless ways to decorate the arrangement, depending upon what shapes you wish to cut out or what fresh herbs or edible flowers you have on hand. This simple preparation is really subject to your whim and whimsy.

Make the marinade the day before you are ready to use it. If you don't have the time, blend all the marinade ingredients except the mushrooms briefly in a blender, but avoid emulsifying the mixture.

Combine the vinegar, oil, salt, sugar, onion, garlic, and mushrooms in a bowl. Stir and allow to sit overnight.

Place an endive on a cutting board with the tapered end facing you. Cut from but not through the base of the endive toward you all the way through the top. Rotate the endive and continue to make these long cuts to shred the endive, keeping the base intact. The cut endive should appear somewhat like a shaving brush. Carefully cut away the browned base of the bottom without cutting across your other slices. Repeat for the other endive.

Place the endive in a bowl and cover with the marinade. Let sit for 2 to 3 minutes.

Remove endive from marinade and place on a plate covered with a paper towel. Pat gently with the towel to remove excess marinade.

Pick up an endive and spread out the "leaves" so that when you place it on the serving plate, it is splayed out over half the plate. Repeat for the other endive. Decorate the endive with the marinated mushrooms, pickled ginger, herbs, and flowers to resemble a flower arrangement.

Halve the plum tomatoes crosswise, then slice the length of each half so you have 4 pieces. Remove pulp and seeds. Cut a zigzag pattern on top half of each piece to create a coarse "saw" pattern and place at the base of each endive.

Serves 4

---

¹⁄₃ cup white wine vinegar

²⁄₃ cup olive oil

¹⁄₂ teaspoon salt

¹⁄₂ teaspoon sugar

¹⁄₃ cup finely chopped onion

1 teaspoon minced garlic

¹⁄₂ cup blanched fresh mushrooms or canned peeled straw mushrooms

4 Belgian endive

4 small pieces pickled ginger, white or red (available in Asian markets)

Assorted fresh herbs, such as savory, thyme, oregano, or basil, and edible flowers, such as pansies or nasturtiums

1 to 2 large plum tomatoes

Pennsylvania Polenta with Sliced Shiitake

Polenta is made with cornmeal, but farina (cream of wheat) is just as versatile. Cooled, sliced, and baked with shiitake, it makes an interesting side dish for any meat.

The polenta can be studded with an endless array of fresh herbs, chopped vegetables, or even meat or fish, and served as a dish by itself with its own sauce. It can be kept for up to a week in the refrigerator.

---

3 ounces fresh shiitake, thinly sliced with stems removed

½ cup farina (cream of wheat)

3 garlic cloves, finely chopped

2 eggs

2 egg yolks

2 tablespoons grated Parmesan cheese

1 tablespoon finely diced red bell pepper

Tabasco sauce

Salt

Place the mushrooms in 2 cups lightly salted water in a medium saucepan and bring to a boil. Simmer for 1 minute, then slowly add the cream of wheat, stirring. Continue to stir gently while the cereal thickens, about 10 minutes. Cereal should become very thick. Remove from the heat and add the garlic, eggs, egg yolks, cheese, red pepper, and Tabasco, and salt to taste, blending thoroughly.

Pour the warm mixture onto a well-oiled baking sheet and spread it out, making the surface as even as possible. Let cool, uncovered, in the refrigerator until cool to the touch.

Remove from the refrigerator and cut into decorative patterns with a cookie cutter. Cover with plastic wrap and refrigerate. When ready to use, place the pieces of polenta on a pan lined with aluminum foil and heat in a 400° F. oven for 5 minutes. Serve immediately.

Serves 6

Caribbean Shiitake

Life is too short to cook too seriously all the time. There are those dishes and those mushrooms we can look fondly upon as opportunities for putting on our culinary polka dot underwear. If food could smile, this is what it would look like. Serve it over rice studded with almonds and golden raisins.

Combine the soy sauce, brown sugar, vinegar, cayenne pepper, ½ cup cold water, and the cornstarch in a small bowl and set aside.

Sauté the scallions and garlic over medium heat in the olive oil in a large sauté pan for

2 tablespoons soy sauce

1 teaspoon brown sugar

2 teaspoons white wine vinegar

¼ teaspoon cayenne pepper

2 teaspoons cornstarch

½ cup medium-sliced scallions, white part only

4 garlic cloves, thinly sliced

1 tablespoon olive oil

18 medium to large fresh shiitake caps, stems removed

½ cup cubed fresh pineapple

½ large red bell pepper, cored and cut into ¼-inch slices

½ cup cubed cooked green banana or plantain

½ cup firmly packed coarsely chopped fresh cilantro

30 seconds. Add the shiitake and continue to sauté for 2 minutes. If the shiitake do not give off any liquid, add about 2 tablespoons water. Stir in the pineapple, red pepper, and banana or plantain. Cover and simmer for 5 minutes.

Add the cilantro and soy sauce mixture slowly while stirring. Heat until the dish is lightly thickened; add a little more water if too thick. Serve immediately.

Serves 4
Suggested wine: Sweet or semisweet Parker Riesling

Bahian Clams

Along the northern coast of Brazil is a city called Salvador, better known as Bahia. It is inhabited by descendants of slaves brought to South America by Portuguese sailors in the late sixteenth century. In a curious manifestation of the tail wagging the dog, Bahian cuisine has had a profound influence on the cooking of Brazil—owing to its intense African flavors. The colors here are bright, the tastes spicy, and the spirit that of energy seasoned with grace.

Dried shiitake can be used for this dish, but you must first reconstitute them in boiling water for about 30 minutes.

THE SAUCE
2 tablespoons white or red wine vinegar

Juice of 1/2 small lemon

1 tablespoon light soy sauce

1 tablespoon sugar

1/2 tablespoon cornstarch

THE CLAMS
3 tablespoons vegetable oil

1 cup mixed thinly sliced bell peppers (green, red, and, if available, yellow and orange peppers)

1/2 cup cubed fresh pineapple

15 small fresh shiitake caps

2 teaspoons finely chopped serrano or jalapeño chiles or equivalent

24 littleneck clams, shucked

1 tablespoon coarsely chopped fresh cilantro, plus sprigs for garnish

To make the sauce, combine 1/4 cup water with the vinegar, lemon juice, soy sauce, sugar, and cornstarch in a cup. Set aside.

Pour the oil into a large saucepan over medium heat. When just barely hot, add the bell peppers, pineapple, shiitake, and chile. Sauté over medium heat until the peppers are tender, 2 to 3 minutes.

Mix the sauce so the cornstarch becomes fully blended with the rest of the sauce. Slowly add to the sauté pan while stirring. It will begin to thicken. Add the clams and the cilantro and stir. Simmer for 30 seconds, then remove from heat. You must be sure the clams do not overcook or they will become tough; they are done when they are still quite raw but just warm in the middle. Divide among 4 plates and garnish with sprigs of cilantro. Serve immediately.

Serves 4

Suggested wine: Gewürztraminer

Coral mushroom

THE BEST OF THE REST

AMONG MUSHROOM HUNTERS HUNCHED
over plates of their favorite fungi, you will often hear arguments over how a mushroom tastes or how one mushroom goes better with meat than another, and so forth. Field guides comment on a mushroom's flavor and sometimes try to fit the taste to the name with hilarious results. For example, I've read that oyster mushrooms have a flavor somewhat resembling oysters, of course (they don't). The name more aptly describes the shape of the mushroom, which resembles the flat side of an oyster shell. Moreover, wild oyster mushrooms are creamy white in color, which you might say makes them resemble the inside of the shell, but that's where the resemblance ends.

But flavor is not the only barometer of interest and quality. Texture plays an important role as well, and often is at least as important as flavor. *Crunchy, chewy,* and *velvety* are words often used to describe the feel of mushrooms in your mouth, and those characteristics determine the suitability of the mushroom for pot or wok. Generally, Americans prefer wild mushrooms that are either crunchy or soft, whereas Asians are fond of textures that are chewy to tough, and flavors that are bitter, such as that of the *Polyporus squamosus* (Dryad's saddle). Whatever your preference, wild mushrooms offer a wide spectrum from which to choose.

The *Russula* Group   Few species of wild mushrooms dot the summer forests with more panache and color than the members of this genus. Delicate and plentiful, they form the palate of a late August day in Berks County, Pennsylvania. The group contains a number of colorful and edible mushrooms, many of which are devilishly difficult to identify. A "red" russula, for example, can be any one of more than twenty species, and except for one or two varieties, we generally ignore them for want of clear identification. The two we do pick are the *R. mariae* and the firmer and meatier *R. subdepalans.* On the West Coast, mushroom hunters pick *R. xerampelina,* known as the shrimp russula, which is also a meaty, red russula.

I use the term "meaty" because that is an unusual characteristic for russulas. They are usually very brittle and are innocent targets for mushroom hunters whose treasures are the more substantial boletes that come up at the same time. Because they crumble so dramatically and into so many pieces, thoughtless hunters love to crush them underfoot and then turn around to admire their terrible handiwork. Poor russulas. That brittleness also makes them difficult to pick and get home in one piece. However, once cooked, they become more elastic and are quite good in casseroles. Good green varieties include *R. virescens* and *R. aeruginea.* Others that we use regularly are the purple *R. cyanoxantha,* the greenish *R. olivacea,* and the white *R. delica.* If you find a quantity of these mushrooms, the best way to preserve them is to blanch them in a pot of boiling water, let them cool in the water, then freeze them, covered with the liquid.

The *Lactarius* Group   These mushrooms are similar to russulas but they ooze a milky substance, hence the generic name. They are rarely brittle like russulas and are generally firmer. The best—such as *L. deliciosus, L. sanguifluus, L. indigo,* and *L. chelidonius*— are quite firm and the object of many forays in Europe. A favorite method the Poles use is to wrap a piece of bacon around the raw cap and put it in the oven for several minutes until the cap and bacon are cooked. They are good candidates for pickling because of their texture. One variety picked extensively in California is *L. camphoratus* (also *L. fragilis),* which when dried has an aroma of maple candy, hence the common name "candy caps." They are used in cakes and cookies. *Lactarius* mushrooms are especially good in stir-fried dishes where distinctive crunchy texture is a real plus.

Coprinus comatus   Common name—inky caps. "Inky" is the way the caps look after they have begun to deliquesce, or to devour themselves from the outer rim toward the center, exuding an ink-like substance in the process. Before that process begins, however, the mushrooms look like shaggy manes, which is another common name. Inky is a name given to the genus as a whole, but most people are referring to this mushroom when they speak of inky caps, because it is the best known. They are best treated very delicately, such as by steaming them very gently after painting the caps with soy sauce, oyster sauce, or other similarly strong, thick sauces. You cannot preserve them in any way. Make sure to cook them soon after picking or they will "ink" in your refrigerator.

Puffballs   Stymied for years by this voluptuous looking fungus, I stumbled upon a method for cooking them one afternoon when I added some shredded *nori,* dried seaweed, to a cream soup I had made with puffballs. I was always put off by their slightly minty character and threw away more than I kept. Until then. From that day I have used *nori* in all of my puffball preparations. The *nori* seems to take that negative residual mintiness off the palate and allows you to enjoy the mushroom. Giant puffballs are of the genus *Calvatia* (*C. gigantea, C. booniana,* and *C. sculpta*). A host of other genera represent everything else. *Calvatia* represents the puffballs most commonly eaten, however. They can grow to five pounds or more. In fact, I have considered some hunts successful when I have returned with just one puffball. They look so eerie, sitting in a forest as if the soil were struck with a magic wand at that spot. When sitting in a well-fertilized field, they look like extraterrestrial growths. As food they are most often compared to tofu, but are a little more assertive on the palate. They can also be sliced and used like eggplant. This is one mushroom where you can go crazy with garlic to your heart's content. I think puffballs are especially good in Japanese preparations where tamari, soy sauce, sake, and mirin are principal ingredients.

Lepiota procera   Common name—parasol mushroom. It's tough to find just one, and tough to find more than three. That's the way *Lepiota procera* grow in Pennsylvania. In our best year, we found about twenty. The stalk is tough, so that leaves you with a meaty, hairy cap that is best breaded and fried. No matter how you cook these mushrooms, don't slice them before you are ready to put them into your mouth, where their delightful springiness will give you a smile and get you hooked on mushroom hunting. Only eat them fresh because they do not preserve very well, although some people enjoy them dried and reconstituted. There is a larger version of this mushroom known as the shaggy or large parasol mushroom, the *L. rachodes,* which is both larger and generally more gregarious than the *L. procera.* They are very similar in character and can be prepared the same way.

Lepista nuda   Common name—blewit, wood blewit. Fruiting from late summer into early December, the blewit is a joy to hunt because success usually means a whole load of fresh mushrooms for supper. The small caps are excellent for pickling and soups and the mature caps, sometimes measuring three to five inches across the top, have great texture and are wonderful sliced into omelets sautéed with red onions and garlic. The large caps can also be grilled after being painted with olive oil and doused with sherry and soy sauce.

The *Tricholoma* Group   The gray members of this group are known as *grizettes* by the French, but I always knew them by their Polish names, *siwki (T. potentossum).* There is also a yellow species, *T. flavovirens,* which we call *gaski.* We find them in pine forests from about the beginning of October into the middle of December. They take on the pine scents of the forest floor from which they spring and are, therefore, similar to matsutake. The delicate fragrance of these mushrooms makes them ideal for clear soups flavored with just a few slices of scallions and several mushroom caps. Since they are often found in good quantity, we usually can or freeze them after blanching. The young caps found early in the season are ideal for pickling, even though they lose their delicate flavor that way. Another European variety is the *T. gambosum,* a white *Tricholoma* that goes by the name of St. George's mushroom.

CLEANING—OR WHY YOU MIGHT THINK I'M CRAZY

When I was little and we would return from a day of successful mushroom hunting in the woods, I could hardly believe my mother's patience as she poured the bushels of mushrooms (usually gaski and siwki) into a large tub and sat and cleaned them for hours until they were ready for blanching and canning. There were times when she would clean from five or six o'clock in the evening until two or three into the next morning. I knew my mother had to be a saint to endure this little-known side of mushroom hunting. As I grew older, my father started to suggest in the strongest terms that, since I was now part of the business, I should take part in getting the mushrooms ready for the kitchen.

You see, cleaning is the nonglamorous part of mushrooming and several bushels of Tricholomas with half a pine forest stuck to their gooey caps and embedded in their gills can be quite daunting, especially after an exhausting day of crawling after them along the forest floor. But there they sit like a basket of dirty beggars waiting to be dressed up, and there is no option but to roll up your sleeves and get to it. The first few times I did it, I realized why everybody wasn't picking wild mushrooms. You have to inspect every cap, stem, and gill for the dirt and insects that miraculously find their way into the mushroom flesh, then remove it or them.

So I would plop myself on a stool over a full tub of mushrooms, and, one by one, begin the process of washing the mushrooms. The first few times were agony because all I could think of was when it would be all over and when I could go to bed. My back would ache and I would grumble when Mom or Pop would evaluate my work the next day and point out all the pine needles I had missed. Oh, God! I frequently thought about running away from home.

Nevertheless, I became reconciled to doing it and I tried a few things to make it less of a drudgery. First, I tried playing music, which helped a little, but soon I had played all my tapes several times and got bored with that. Then I thought a glass or two of wine would make it easier. Big mistake! The day's exhaustion from picking would well up after the first glass and my eyelids would suddenly feel as if they were made of cement. Finally I tried doing some projects in my head pertaining to the business while cleaning the mushrooms, just to get my mind off what I was doing. Then a funny thing happened. I began peering down at the individual mushrooms I was cleaning and began noticing things, like how different they were from one another or how the slightly viscous caps of the mushrooms would feel pleasantly slippery in my fingers like shiny little bald heads of wood elfins. Then I would get a small twinge of satisfaction as I transformed each one from a crummy urchin into a cleaned and spiffy-looking dandy ready for the most aristocratic of dishes.

I would subdivide the most perfect caps into separate pots just for pickling. These would later go into our Martinis at Joe's. The larger "meat" caps would be used for casseroles, while others would be used for soups. Then I understood everything. I understood how Mom and Pop could do this for hours, and how, when I peered into the mass of mushrooms and really began to concentrate on what I was doing, I could get hooked on this. Where else can you get such a delightful appreciation of nature reinforced by the tactile sensation of rolling your fingertips over a perfectly formed cap? Like people, each one is different. But the interesting part is that the mushrooms hadn't changed, and the dirt was still there, and it still took long hours to get them cleaned. No, the difference was in me and how my perception changed to make this one of my favorite activities. So now, when I have full baskets to clean, and my parents volunteer to do it for me at their house, I tell them, "No, that's okay. I'll do it." There is a regretful pause, and I know what they're thinking, so I say, "All right, I'll split them with you. What time can I bring them up?"

Edible *Amanitas*   *Amanita* is the genus that contains the deadliest of the poisonous mushrooms. It also contains some of the finest wild mushrooms in the forest, among them the *A. caesarea,* the famed Caesar's mushroom, which can trace its culinary history back to ancient times. As you sauté this mushroom it creates its own red-orange sauce, and it is delicious. Some quantities of this mushroom in its completely closed stage are shipped in from Italy. They look like little furry eggs wrapped in their delicate sheath and are highly prized. Other species are also enjoyed, such as the *A. calyptrata (coccora, coccoli), A. vaginata (grizette),* and *A. velosa.* You must be an expert mushroom hunter, however, to ever take the chance of picking and eating these on your own. The mushrooms are best enjoyed alone because of their delicate flavor and do not respond well to any form of preservation, so eat them while you have them.

Marasmius oreades   Common name—fairy ring mushroom, *mousseron.* The fairy ring mushroom is widely enjoyed because of its abundance and relative ease of identification. I find it pleasant but not really worth the enthusiasm of other mushroom hunters. One of its defining characteristics is its ability to reconstitute almost fully having been dried. Big deal. The stem is too tough to eat and you do need a good mouthful of these mushrooms to be satisfied. As you might expect, drying is the preferred method of preservation. These mushrooms are good enhancers for stews and light soups, and are also good in scrambled eggs.

Lyophyllum descastes   Common name—fried chicken mushroom. This is another head-scratcher in regards to the name. It has a mild flavor at best, with really no resemblance to fried chicken, but it is commonly picked and eaten because it grows in abundance. This mushroom is available from time to time on the wholesale wild mushroom market.

Hypomyces lactifluorum   Common name—lobster mushroom. No, this mushroom doesn't taste like lobster, but its color is that of a cooked lobster. Lobster mushrooms have a pleasant crunchy texture, which is interesting because they are actually delicate mushrooms (usually of the genus *Russula*) that are parasitized by the genus *Hypomyces,* with the result that the delicate character of the *Russulas* are completely transformed. The *Hypomyces* can parasitize just about any mushroom, so many hunters stay away from them because they might be parasitic on a poisonous mushroom. On the other hand, lobster mushrooms from the Pacific Northwest are sold commercially in large quantities and there have not been, to my knowledge, any reported cases of poisoning from them. They are quite popular because of their red-orange color and crunchy texture, which are always welcome in a dish.

Dentinum (also *Hydnum*) *repandum, D. umbilicatum*   Common name—hedgehog, sweet tooth, *pied-de-mouton,* wood urchin, pig's trotter. Out of the gloom of eastern winters, when mushroom hunters and chefs fret awaiting rebirth of the earth, comes this harbinger. It is the one mushroom available from the Pacific Northwest at a time when everything else seems to be resting underground. It is the mushroom we use in January and February, when even black chanterelles from Oregon and Washington are scarce. And welcome they are in our kitchen. You might even call this odd mushroom a winter chanterelle, because it resembles chanterelles in color and even in flavor, although it is an unusual mushroom because it has "teeth" hanging from the underside of the cap instead of pores or gills. The body of the mushroom is fairly delicate and tends to break apart in transit. They can be used in the same way as chanterelles and can be preserved by canning.

Rosites caperata   Common name—gypsy. Another mushroom usually picked in quantity, it is generally more popular in Europe than in North America. The stems are tough but the caps are fleshy and very good for sautéing with veal or beef. Canning is the only way to preserve these mushrooms.

Huitlacoche (also cuitlacoche) *Ustilago maydis*   Common name—Corn smut. In Mayan, *huitlacoche* means "Food of the Gods." It is considered a delicacy in Mexico, where its growth is encouraged by scratching the base of the cornstalk and piling soil against the scratch to introduce the spores. (In eastern Pennsylvania, shocked farmers can't believe we want to eat it.) *Huitlacoche* has a mild fungal flavor not unlike the button mushroom. It produces swollen corn kernels that are blue-grey in color and is available frozen and, sometimes, canned. It requires several minutes of sautéing and mixes well with onions, herbs, and peppers.

Kombucha   Known as the Manchurian mushroom, kombucha has been around for hundreds, maybe thousands, of years. Its popularity comes and goes, yet it endures. It is purported to heal everything from cancer to AIDS. It is not a mushroom, but is rather a blob-like conglomeration of several yeasts and bacteria. It apparently produces a powerful antibiotic, which is the source of its alleged powers. Because it is a microorganism, however, it is susceptible to contamination from other funguses, which makes it a potential health hazard.

Russulas *in Red Pepper Sauce*

Any other wild or domestic mushroom can be used for this recipe as well.

Preheat the oven to 350° F.

Bring about 3 quarts of lightly salted water to a boil. Add the potatoes, cover, and cook until the potatoes are soft when pierced with a fork, about 15 minutes.

Place the red peppers in the oven on a baking sheet. Roast until the skins start to wrinkle and darken, 10 to 12 minutes. Some parts of the skin will blacken before the entire peppers are roasted. Remove the peppers from the oven, place in a paper bag, and let sit for 5 minutes, then rub off the skins with a towel, peeling off as much as you can. Split the peppers and remove the seeds and stems. Place the peppers along with the lemon juice, sugar, and ½ teaspoon of salt into a blender and process until smooth. Work this puree through a sieve to remove any bits of skin. Set aside.

Drain the potatoes, place in a food processor, and process until well pureed, stopping occasionally to wipe down the sides with a rubber spatula. Place the potatoes in the blender and add the cream and milk. Blend until the mixture is smooth, adding a little more milk, if necessary, until the mixture has the consistency of a thickened sauce rather than mashed potatoes. Pour mixture through a medium-fine sieve to eliminate lumps.

4 small new potatoes or 2 russet potatoes, peeled and cut in half

2 large red bell peppers

3 tablespoons fresh lemon juice

1 tablespoon sugar

Salt

¼ cup heavy cream

¼ cup milk, or more as needed

3 chipotle peppers in adobo sauce, pureed

2 tablespoons olive oil

1 small onion, sliced

1 small green bell pepper, thinly sliced

12 ounces fresh russulas, preferably large ones (2 inches or larger cap width), cleaned

Place the sauce in a small saucepan and put over medium heat, stirring. Add the pepper puree and blend well. Add the chipotle puree and blend again. Adjust for salt if necessary. Remove from the heat and keep the sauce warm.

In a large sauté pan, heat the olive oil and add the onion and green pepper. Sauté for 1 minute, then add the mushrooms. Sauté until the mushrooms go limp and the excess liquid has evaporated, about 2 minutes. Season with salt to taste.

Evenly divide the warmed sauce among 4 plates, covering the plates generously. Arrange the sautéed mushrooms in the middle and serve immediately.

Serves 4
Suggested wine: Stag's Leap Wine Cellar's Reserve Chardonnay

Venison with Wood Blewits and Cardamom Sauce

Blewits have a mild flavor that is perked up by this sauce.

Preheat the oven to 450° F.

Place the venison on a work surface and press the flour mixture all over the surface of the meat. Add a few tablespoons of oil to a large sauté pan and turn the heat to high. When the oil begins to smoke, add the venison and brown for 1 minute, then turn it 45 degrees, brown again, then again twice more until the venison is browned all over. This should take no longer than 5 minutes.

Place the venison on a rack with a pan underneath to catch any drippings. Put in the oven and roast for 12 to 15 minutes, so the venison is rare to medium-rare. Test by plunging a fork into the middle of the loin. The temperature should be noticeably warm without being hot.

While the venison is roasting, prepare the

2 pound loin of venison, free of fat, bone, or sinew

⅓ cup all-purpose flour mixed with 1 teaspoon each salt and pepper

Vegetable oil

1 large yellow or red onion, sliced

10 ounces fresh wood blewits or any other fresh mushroom, cleaned

½ teaspoon salt

Sugar

1 tablespoon light soy sauce

½ cup dry red wine

1 tablespoon dark soy sauce

2 teaspoons ground cardamom

1 teaspoon arrowroot mixed with ⅓ cup cold water

mushrooms. Add 2 tablespoons of the oil to a large sauté pan. Add the onion and sauté for 1 minute. Add the mushrooms and sauté until the mushrooms have become limp and most of the liquid has evaporated, about 8 minutes. Add the salt, ½ teaspoon sugar, and the light soy sauce and blend well. Set aside and keep warm.

To make the sauce, combine the wine, 2 tablespoons of sugar, the dark soy sauce, cardamom, and ½ cup of water in a small saucepan. Bring to a simmer, then add the arrowroot mixture and stir until the sauce just begins to thicken. Keep warm.

Remove the venison from the oven and slice into 4 pieces. Distribute the mushrooms on 4 plates, place a slice of venison over them, cover with the sauce, and serve.

Serves 4
Suggested wine: Cabernet Sauvignon

Filet of Sole with Hericium and Tangerine Peel

Any of the more delicate-fleshed fish in the sole family can be used in this recipe, along with bass or trout.

Preheat the oven to 450° F.

Lay out 4 pieces of parchment paper or aluminum foil about 15 inches long by 8 inches wide. Place with the vertical length facing you. Oil the bottom half of the paper or foil, then place a filet on each piece. Sprinkle the fish liberally with the wine and butter, then lightly salt. Sprinkle with the tangerine peel, then rub it in so that each filet is evenly covered. Cover each filet with some sliced red pepper, then with the sliced mushrooms. Finally, lightly salt the mushrooms.

Fold the parchment or foil in half over each filet. Fold to enclose, then fold over either side so that the filets are entirely enclosed. Place on a baking sheet and bake for 10 minutes. Remove from the oven, place on serving plates, and serve.

---

4 filets of sole, about 5 ounces each

Dry white wine

Melted butter

Salt

1/2 teaspoon grated tangerine peel

1 red bell pepper, seeded, cored, and thinly sliced

4 ounces fresh Hericium, cleaned and thinly sliced

Serves 4

Suggested wine: David Bruce Chardonnay

Ragout of Hedgehog Mushrooms with Tangerines and Curry

(photograph opposite)

Tangerines give this dish a citrusy burst in the mouth.

Place the oil in a large saucepan over medium heat. Add the onions and sauté until just barely soft, about 3 minutes. Add the mushrooms and continue to sauté for 5 minutes more.

Add the orange juice, savory, curry powder, and salt, and heat for 1 minute. Add the cream and heat until the mixture begins to thicken. Add the tangerine sections and heat for 2 minutes more. The mixture should be thickened enough so that the sauce does not run. If not, continue to heat until it reaches that point. Serve immediately.

Serves 4
Suggested wine: Riesling

> 3 tablespoons extra-virgin olive oil
> 2 small onions, finely chopped
> 1 pound fresh hedgehog mushrooms
> Juice of 1 orange
> ½ teaspoon dried savory
> 1 teaspoon curry powder
> 1 teaspoon salt
> ¾ cup heavy cream
> 3 tangerines, peeled and sectioned into small pieces, pith removed as best as possible

Parasol Mushroom Fritters

Other mushrooms with larger caps can be used in this recipe, but those caps should not exceed three or four inches in diameter.

In a large saucepan, heat the oil to 375° F.

While the oil is heating, combine the egg, milk, cream, salt, sugar, soy sauce, pepper, cayenne, and flour in a mixing bowl with 2 tablespoons of water. Blend well with a whisk. Dip the mushroom caps in the batter and fry until light golden, 2 at a time, about 45 seconds. Drain the fried mushrooms on paper towels, place them on a serving plate, and serve while still hot.

Serves 4
Suggested wine: Byron Pinot Noir

> About 2 quarts vegetable oil, for frying
> 1 egg
> 1 tablespoon milk
> 1 tablespoon heavy cream
> ½ teaspoon salt
> ½ teaspoon sugar
> ½ teaspoon soy sauce
> Pinch of black pepper
> Pinch of cayenne pepper
> ½ cup all-purpose flour
> 4 large or 6 to 8 small fresh parasol mushroom caps
> (Lepiota procera)

Confit of Amanita Caesarea *and Red Onions on Fried Bread*

In this recipe, the Amanitas are sautéed in plenty of butter and served over bread fried in fritter batter. Other mushrooms may be substituted, but only the Amanita caesarea will give off its characteristic reddish "sauce."

Place the butter in a large sauté pan over high heat. Add the onions and sauté for 1 minute. Add the coriander, chili powder, garlic, lemon juice, pepper, red wine, 1 teaspoon of the salt, 1 teaspoon of the sugar, 1 tablespoon of the soy sauce, and the mushrooms and sauté until the mushrooms go limp and begin to release their liquid, about 6 minutes. Simmer until most but not all of the liquid has evaporated. Keep warm.

⅓ cup butter
2 large red onions, peeled and thinly sliced
½ teaspoon ground coriander
½ teaspoon chili powder
1 teaspoon minced garlic
1 teaspoon lemon juice
¼ teaspoon black pepper
2 tablespoons dry red wine
1½ teaspoons salt
1½ teaspoons sugar
3½ teaspoons soy sauce
1 pound fresh Amanita caesarea, cleaned but with stems on
About 1 quart vegetable oil, for frying
1 egg
1 tablespoon milk
1 tablespoon heavy cream
Pinch of black pepper
Pinch of cayenne pepper
½ cup all-purpose flour
4 pieces French bread, in 1-inch-thick slices

In a large saucepan, heat the oil to 375° F.

While the oil is heating, combine the egg, milk, cream, ½ teaspoon of salt, ½ teaspoon of sugar, ½ teaspoon of soy sauce, the cayenne and black peppers, 2 tablespoons of water, and the flour in a mixing bowl, and blend well with a whisk. Coat the pieces of bread completely with the batter and fry until light golden in the oil, 2 pieces at a time, about 45 seconds. Drain the fried bread on a paper towel and place each in the middle of a plate. Cover each piece of fried bread with some of the confit and serve.

Serves 4
Suggested wine: Muscat di Canelli

Three-Mushroom Tart with Clitopilus prunulis and Honey Mushrooms

The magic in any good tart or quiche is in the custard. The custard here is enriched with cèpes. You may, however, use any mushrooms you please in the tart itself, but softer, more pliable varieties are best for overall texture. This recipe is one of Heidi's.

Mix the flour and salt in a large bowl. Cut the lard or margarine into the flour with a pastry cutter, add ⅓ cup cold water, and mix until a ball is formed from the dough. Chill for 30 minutes.

Preheat the oven to 375° F.

Roll out the dough and lay into a 10-inch springform pan along the bottom and up the sides. Press foil onto the dough and weight with some uncooked beans or rice. Place into the oven and bake for 10 minutes. Remove from oven, remove beans, and let cool.

Add the butter to a large sauté pan over medium heat and sauté the onion for 1 minute.

Add the mushrooms and red pepper and continue to sauté for another 2 minutes. Add the garlic, curry powder, savory, and cayenne; stir well, and remove from the heat and let cool.

Beat the eggs with a whisk in a bowl and add the cream, whisking well. Add the mushroom mixture to the custard and mix again.

Pour the custard mixture into the pastry shell and bake for 15 minutes, then turn down the heat to 300° F. and bake until custard sets, about another 15 minutes, or until a fork inserted in the center comes out clean. Let stand for 15 minutes, then slice and serve.

Serves 8 to 10

Suggested wine: A big, woody Chardonnay, such as Edna Valley

THE TART CRUST
2 cups all-purpose flour
1 teaspoon salt
10 tablespoons lard or margarine

THE FILLING
3 tablespoons butter
1 medium onion, finely chopped
2 cups chopped Clitopilus prunulis
1 cup reconstituted cèpes, finely chopped
1 cup sliced fresh honey mushrooms
¼ cup chopped red bell pepper
1 teaspoon minced garlic
½ teaspoon curry powder
½ teaspoon dried savory
Pinch of cayenne pepper
4 eggs
2 cups heavy cream

Inky Caps Steamed with Oyster Sauce and Ginger

Inky caps (Coprinus comatus) *are plentiful in the fall in eastern Pennsylvania. They are also notoriously delicate and tricky to handle. Over the years I have found that steaming is the best way to prepare them without damaging the delicate beauty and shape of the closed caps.*

For a little zing, add some chile oil (available in Asian markets) to the oyster sauce.

Lay the mushrooms out on a dinner plate that will fit inside your steamer. Combine the ginger with the oyster sauce and, with a pastry brush, carefully paint each cap with the sauce, turning the caps as you work.

Place about 2 inches of water in the bottom of a steamer. Bring the water to a boil. Lay the plate with the mushrooms on the rack above the simmer-ing water. Place the lid of the steamer tightly over the top and let mushrooms steam for 5 minutes. Carefully remove and serve.

Serves 4
Suggested wine: Ravenswood Zinfandel

---

12 to 15 Inky caps, stems cleaned and free of dirt
1 teaspoon finely chopped fresh ginger
⅓ cup Chinese oyster sauce

Consommé of Grizettes

The genus Tricholoma contains some of the most prolific mushrooms in the forest. We pick the ones that grow in pine forests in the fall, which have a resinous or piney flavor that is the substance of its charm. The flavor is distinct and so this recipe is "mushroom specific."

Shiitake can be substituted, but will produce, of course, a very different consommé. Also, this recipe can easily be made in a microwave. Simply place the mushrooms and 2 cups of water in a microwave-safe bowl and place in the microwave.

---

1 cup tiny
Tricholoma portentosum *caps*
Salt
*1 tablespoon very thinly sliced
scallion, white part only*

Bring to a boil several times. Remove, season with salt, and add the scallions.

In a small saucepan, combine the mushrooms and 2 cups of water. Bring the mushrooms to a boil, then simmer for 10 minutes. Remove from the heat and season to taste with salt. Add the scallions and ladle into bowls to serve.

Serves 4

Puffball Soup

Puffballs are very popular among mushroom hunters, but I find them tricky to work with. They respond well to seaweed; the texture and flavor of the seaweed seems to mute the "minty" character of puffballs.

Place the butter in a large saucepan over medium heat. Add the onion and sauté until lightly browned, about 5 minutes.

⅓ cup butter
1 large onion, finely chopped
*4 cups chopped fresh puffballs,
in ½-inch cubes*
2 cups heavy cream
2 cups milk
*3 tablespoons dried loose seaweed,
such as nori (available in
Asian markets)*
Salt

Add the puffballs and sauté for 5 minutes more. The puffballs will release some liquid.

Add the cream, milk, and seaweed. Simmer for another 20 minutes. The soup will thicken slightly. Salt to taste and serve.

Serves 8 to 10

Suggested wine: Buena Vista Gamay Beaujolais

Mexican Calzone

For those who enjoy making your own bread, tear off a piece of dough and try this. It can satisfy legions of hungry waifs waiting for hot, oven-fresh bread. Standard white bread dough is safest for this calzone. Dense, whole wheat breads can become crumbly. You can really use any filling you like, and wild mushrooms work particularly well, but the texture of huitlacoche, an edible corn fungus, is best for this preparation.

Preheat the oven to 400° F.

Heat the oil in a large saucepan over medium heat. Add the onion and sauté for 2 minutes. Add the *huitlacoche* and sauté until it is tender, about 2 minutes. Season with salt to taste. Remove from the heat and stir in the cilantro and truffle oil. Let cool.

---

2 tablespoons vegetable oil
1 large red onion, sliced
8 ounces huitlacoche, *cleaned*
Salt
2 tablespoons finely chopped fresh cilantro
1 tablespoon truffle oil (optional; available at specialty markets)
1 pound bread dough, in 4 pieces
3 chipotle peppers, pureed
4 ounces Mexican Chihuahua cheese or Monterey Jack, grated or sliced

---

Roll out each piece of dough on a well-floured wooden surface so that it is roughly round and with a 4-to-6-inch diameter. Spread one fourth of the chipotle puree evenly over the surface of each dough. Mound some of the filling in the center, then top each with one fourth of the cheese. Fold the dough over the filling once so that the opposite sides are touching, a half-moon. Crimp and fold the touching edges together to seal the calzone completely. Place in the oven and bake for 10 minutes, or until calzones are browned and hot. Remove from the oven and let rest for 5 minutes before serving.

Serves 4
Suggested accompaniment: Mexican beer

Grilled Filet of Shark with Venison-Lactarius Duxelles

Big-bodied fish—such as shark and tuna—have the ability to stand up to meat flavors. This liberated version of duxelles acts as a foil for the fish.

Swordfish can also be used, however the mushrooms should be of the firm variety, which is why Lactarius is used. If you use another variety (say, domestic), they must be cooked only briefly.

Prepare a charcoal grill or preheat the broiler.

Brush the fish with some soy sauce and let stand for 10 minutes. Grill or broil the fish until flaky, about 3 minutes. Keep warm.

Heat a wok or sauté pan. Add the peanut oil and then the scallions, and sauté for 30 seconds.

---

4 filets of shark, 6 to 8 ounces each

Soy sauce

3 tablespoons peanut oil

4 scallions, white parts only, cut into 1-inch pieces

½ ounce fresh ginger, sliced thin, then cut into ¼-inch sticks

6 ounces fresh Lactarius, cleaned and sliced

4 ounces lean venison, sliced to approximate the mushroom slices

2 tablespoons hoisin sauce

Add the ginger and sauté for another minute. Add the mushrooms and sauté for 2 minutes more. Finally, add the venison and sauté until the meat just begins to turn color, about 3 minutes. You do not want the meat to be overdone, rather it should be rare to medium rare inside, so cook it very briefly.

Stirring, add the hoisin sauce to the meat and mushroom mixture. Remove from the heat and divide evenly onto 4 plates. Cover with the grilled fish and serve.

Serves 4

Suggested wine: Petit Sirah

It is the early morning. The gray light just begins to frame the drawn shades of my bedroom window when I realize that I've been awakened by the thump! thump! thump! of booted feet on a carpeted stairway leading to our front door. Then the door opens and slams just a little harder than it needs to. The boots are now running along the cement, and as I get up from the bed and peek through the shades, the boots arrive at a Ford Bronco with the engine running. Inside I can see the familiar profile of my father staring out, unaware that he is being watched. He is eighty-two and I can just sense in his expression, from that distance, his anticipation of another mushroom adventure in the woods with his grandson Stefan, age twelve. Stefan hops into the Bronco and slams the door. They remain sitting there for a moment, and I know that my father is checking to see if Stefan is dressed properly, has his Buck knife, and has told his mother or father when he will be back. Usually two out of three of the above are sufficient for the expedition to begin.

APPENDIX

ACKNOWLEDGMENTS

FIRST AND FOREMOST, I must acknowledge the support and love of my wife, Heidi, whose patience with me during the writing of this book was nothing less than heroic. Moreover, she contributed several terrific recipes. She continues to amaze me with her natural talent and easy way with food, not to mention her astute criticisms and observations.

My thanks also to my children—Sonja, Chris, and Stefan—who have gone mushroom hunting with us with enthusiasm, always returning upbeat and usually with a load of mushrooms. I cherish their natural curiosity and companionship.

To my father, for introducing me not only to mushrooms but to a way of life in this business we love. His passion for mushrooms and fine cooking finally rubbed off on me, as did his belief in family and honor, the pillars of a full life.

To my mother, who has—in her quiet and wise fashion—provided love and sustenance to our family for three generations. A woman of great beauty and insight, she has shone like a fiery star over us all and cast her light so that we might be as tall and great shadows on this earth.

Special thanks to some close friends, Jim and Nan Morrissey and Mike and M. L. Riley, who not only tried many of these dishes but also staged many emergency wine tastings and dinners to help Heidi and me to get away from it all.

To Paul Stamets, whose help was invaluable, especially in researching some of the more esoteric aspects of the fungal world.

To many others whose publications or books were invaluable as sources—especially David Arora, Gary Lincoff, and Orson Miller. Also, special thanks to Jim Angelucci and Craig Handley, two friends who also happen to be experts in the cultivation of mushrooms.

To those whose books and recipes have kept the fungal fires alive in the breasts of mushroom hunters everywhere, especially Larry Stickney for his great columns in *Mushroom, The Journal;* to David Fischer and Arleen and Alan Bessette for their great cookbooks; to Don Coombs, Maggy Rogers, Sam Ristich, and all the others whose passion for mushrooms has inspired me for life.

To my agent Judith Weber, my editor, Ann ffolliott, and my publisher, Leslie Stoker, who so thoroughly—and with great diplomacy—cleaned the literary smudges from my manuscript. My thanks also to Lou Wallach, Hope Koturo, Jim Wageman, and Beth Wareham.

Finally to my staff at Joe's Restaurant and Joe's Bistro—especially Joe Morrissey and Marina Attili—who have helped to keep the engines running smoothly these many years. And to our loyal customers, who have inspired yet more investigation and experimentation into the world of mushroom cookery!

CONVERSIONS

INGREDIENTS AND EQUIPMENT GLOSSARY

British English and American English are not always the same, particularly in the kitchen. The following ingredients and equipment used in this book are pretty much the same on both sides of the Atlantic, but have different names:

American	British
beets	beetroots
Belgian endive	chicory
bell pepper	sweet pepper (capsicum)
broiler/to broil	grill/to grill
confectioners' sugar	icing sugar
cornstarch	cornflour
heavy cream (37.6% fat)	double cream (35–40% fat)
scallion	spring onion
skillet	frying pan

VOLUME EQUIVALENTS

These are not exact equivalents for the American cups and spoons, but have been rounded up or down slightly to make measuring easier.

American	Metric	Imperial
¼ t	1.25 ml	
½ t	2.5 ml	
1 t	5 ml	
½ T (1½ t)	7.5 ml	
1 T (3 t)	15 ml	
¼ cup (4 T)	60 ml	2 fl oz
⅓ cup (5 T)	75 ml	2½ fl oz
½ cup (8 T)	125 ml	4 fl oz
⅔ cup (10 T)	150 ml	5 fl oz (¼ pint)
¾ cup (12 T)	175 ml	6 fl oz
1 cup (16 T)	250 ml	8 fl oz
1¼ cups	300 ml	10 fl oz
1½ cups	350 ml	12 fl oz
1 pint (2 cups)	500 ml	16 fl oz
1 quart (4 cups)	1 litre	1¾ pints

WEIGHT EQUIVALENTS

The metric weights given in this chart are not exact equivalents, but have been rounded up or down slightly to make measuring easier.

Avoirdupois	Metric
¼ oz	7 g
½ oz	15 g
1 oz	30 g
2 oz	60 g
3 oz	90 g
4 oz	115 g
5 oz	150 g
6 oz	175 g
7 oz	200 g
8 oz (½ lb)	225 g
9 oz	250 g
10 oz	300 g
11 oz	325 g
12 oz	350 g
13 oz	375 g
14 oz	400 g
15 oz	425 g
16 oz (1 lb)	450 g
1 lb 2 oz	500 g
1½ lb	750 g
2 lb	900 g
2¼ lb	1 kg
3 lb	1.4 kg
4 lb	1.8 kg
4½ lb	2 kg

OVEN TEMPERATURE EQUIVALENTS

Oven	°F.	°C.	Gas Mark
very cool	250–300	130–150	½–1
cool	300	150	2
warm	325	170	3
moderate	350	180	4
moderately hot	375	190	5
	400	200	6
hot	425	220	7
very hot	450	230	8
	475	250	9

BUTTER

Some confusion may arise over the measuring of butter and other hard fats. In the United States, butter is generally sold in a one-pound package, which contains four equal "sticks." The wrapper on each stick is marked to show tablespoons, so the cook can cut the stick according to the quantity required. The equivalent weights are:

1 stick = 115 g/4 oz
1 T = 15 g/½ oz

FLOUR

American all-purpose flour is milled from a mixture of hard and soft wheats, whereas British plain flour is made mainly from soft wheat. To achieve a near equivalent to American all-purpose flour, use half British plain flour and half strong bread flour.

SUGAR

In the recipes in this book, if sugar is called for, it is assumed to be granulated, unless otherwise specified. American granulated sugar is finer than British granulated, closer to caster sugar.

MAIL-ORDER SOURCES

ADRIANA'S CARAVAN
409 Vanderbilt Street
Brooklyn, NY 11218
800-316-0820
718-436-8565

AUX DELICES DES BOIS, INC.
4 Leonard Street
New York, NY 10013
212-334-1230
FAX 212-334-1231

DELFTREE FARM
234 Union Street
North Adams, MA 01247
800-243-3742
FAX 413-664-4908

FESTIVE FOODS OF THE
ROCKIES, INC.
P.O. Box 49172
Colorado Springs, CO 80949
719-594-6768
FAX 719-522-1672

FUNGI PERFECTI
STAMETS CULTURE COLLECTION
P.O. Box 7634
Olympia, WA 98507
206-426-9292
800-780-9126
FAX 206-426-9377

HANS JOHANSSON'S MUSHROOMS
AND MORE
P.O. Box 532
Goldens Bridge, NY 10526
914-232-2107

PAPRIKAS WEISS IMPORTER
1572 Second Avenue
New York, NY 10028
212/288-6117
FAX 212/734-5120

PHILLIPS MUSHROOM PLACE
909 East Baltimore Pike
Kennett Square, PA 19348
800-243-8644

BIBLIOGRAPHY

Ainsworth, G. D. *Dictionary of the Fungi.* Kew, Surrey: Commonwealth Mycological Institute, 1971.

Alexopoulos, C. J. *Introductory Mycology.* Minneapolis: Burgess Publishing Co., 1972.

————. *Laboratory Manual for Introductory Mycology.* Minneapolis: Burgess Publishing Co., 1962.

Atkinson, G. F. *Mushrooms: Edible and Poisonous.* New York: Hafner Publishing Co., 1961.

Berger, Dr. Karl. *Mykologisches Worterbuch in Acht Sprachen.* Jena: Verlag Gustav Fischer, 1980.

Bessey, E. A. *Morphology and Taxonomy of Fungi.* New York: Hafner Publishing Co., 1961.

Bigelow, H. E., and H. D. Thiers. *Studies on Higher Fungi.* Vaduz: J. Cramer, 1975.

Cash, Edith H. *A Mycological English-Latin Glossary.* New York: Hafner Publishing Co., 1965.

Cernhorski and Machura. *Pilzbibel: Markt und Giftpilze.* Vienna: Verlag Karl Kuhne, 1947.

Clemencon, Heinz. *Les Quatre Saisons des Champignons,* 2 vols. Lausanne: Piantanida, 1980.

Clements, Frederic E., and Cornelius L. Shear. *The Genera of Fungi.* New York: Hafner Publishing Co., 1931.

Coker, W. C. *The Club and Coral Mushrooms of the United States.* New York: Dover reprint, 1974.

Coker, W. C., and J. N. Couch. *The Gastromycetes of the United States.* Chapel Hill: University of North Carolina Press, 1928; New York: Dover reprint, 1974.

Corner, E. J. H. *A Monograph of Thelephora.* Berlin: J. Cramer, 1968.

Costantin, M. J., and M. L. DuFour. *Nouvelle Flore des Champignons.* Paris: Librarie Générale de l'Enseignement, 1947.

Dahnke, R. M., and S. M. Dahnke. 700 *Pilze in Farben.* Stuttgart: A. T. Verlag Aarau, 1980.

Erhart, Josef, and Marie Erhartova. *Houby ve Forografii.* Prague: Statni Zemedelske Nakladatelstvi, 1977.

Farlow, William G. *Icones Farlowianae.* Cambridge, Mass.: The Farlow Herbarium and Library, 1929.

Findlay, W. P. K. *Wayside and Woodland Fungi.* London: F. Warne and Co., 1967.

Gerhardt, Ewald. *Pilzfuhrer.* Munich: BIV Verlagsgesellschaft, 1981.

Guillot, Jean. *Les Champignons.* Paris: Fernand Nathan, 1983.

Guirard, Irena. *Grzyby i Potrawy z Grzybow.* Warsaw: Panstwowe Wydawnictwo Gospodarcze, 1956.

Guminska, Barbara, and Wladyslaw Wojewod. *Grzyby Owocnikowe i ich Oznaczania.* Warsaw: Panstwowe Wydawnictwo Rolnicze i Lesne, 1968.

Gussow, H. T., and W. S. Odell. *Mushrooms and Toadstools.* Ottawa: F. A. Acland, 1927.

Guzman, Gaston. *The Genus Psilocybe.* Vaduz: J. Cramer, 1983.

Haas, H., and G. Gossner. *Pilze Mitteleuropas.* Stuttgart: Frankische Verlagshandlung, 1966.

Halling, Roy E. *The Genus Collybia.* Braunschweig: J. Cramer, 1983.

Hawksworth, D. L., B. C. Sutton, and G. C. Ainsworth. *Ainsworth and Bisby's Dictionary of the Fungi.* Kew, Surrey: Commonwealth Mycological Institute, 1983.

Hawlik, W. J. *Waldpilzzucht fur jedermann.* Munich: Verlag Dr. Richter, 1983.

Hesler, L. R., and A. H. Smith. *North American Species of Hygrophorus.* Knoxville: University of Tennessee Press, 1963.

————. *North American Species of Lactarius.* Ann Arbor: University of Michigan Press, 1979.

Jahn, H. *Mitteleuropaische Porlinge.* Berlin: J. Cramer, 1970.

Jenkins, D. T. *A Taxonomic and Nomenclatural Study of the Genus Amanita. Section Amanita for North America.* Vaduz: J. Cramer, 1977.

Kaufman, C. H. *The Agaricaceae of Michigan,* 2 vols. New York: Johnson Reprint, 1981.

Kavaler, Lucy. *Mushrooms, Molds, and Miracles.* New York: John Day, 1965.

Kleijn, Von H. *Grosses Fotobuch der Pilze.* Garden City, N.Y.: Doubleday, 1962.

————. *Mushrooms and Other Fungi— Their Form and Color.* New York: Doubleday, 1962.

Kornerup, A., and J. H. Wanscher. *Methuen Handbook of Color.* London: Methuen and Co., 1963.

Kreisel, H. *Grundzeuge Eines Naturlichen Systems der Pilze.* Berlin: J. Cramer, 1969.

Krieger, Louis C. *The Mushroom Handbook.* New York: Dover, 1967.

Kuhner, R., and H. Romagnesi. *Flore Analytique des Champignons Supérieurs.* Paris, Masson et Cie., 1953.

Langa, J. E., and M. Lange. 600 *Pilze in Farben.* Munich: BIV Verlagsgesellschaft, 1961.

Meixner, A. *Chemische Farbreaktionen von Pilzen.* Vaduz: J. Cramer, 1975.

Michael, Edmund, Bruno Hennig, and Hanns Kreisel. *Handbuch fur Pilzfreunde,* 4 vols. Jena: Verlag Gustav Fischer, 1977.

Moser, Meinhard. *Agarics and Boleti.* London: Phillips, 1983.

Needham, G. H. *The Microscope.* Springfield, Ill.: Charles Thomas, 1968.

Nespiak, Andrzej. *Grzyby (Mycota) Tom VII: Basidiomycetes, Agaricales, Cortinariaceae, Cortinarius.* Warsaw: Panstwowe Wydawnictwo Naukowe, 1975.

Peck, Charles H. *Memoir of The New York State Museum.* Albany: State University of New York, 1900.

Phillips, Roger. *Mushrooms and Other Fungi of Great Britain and Europe.* London: Ward Lock, 1981.

Pilat, Albert. *Mushrooms.* London: Spring Books, n.d.

————. *Mushrooms and Other Fungi.* London: Peter Neville, 1961.

Pilat, Albert, and O. Usak. *Maty Atlas Grzybow.* Warsaw: Panstwowe Wydawnictwo Rolnicae i Lesne, 1978.

Pomerleau, Rene. *Les Amanites du Quebec.* Quebec: Naturaliste, 1966.

Rayner, R. W. *A Mycological Color Chart.* Kew, Surrey: Commonwealth Mycological Institute, 1970.

Richter, J. *Austernpilz Kochbuch.* Munich: Verlag Dr. Richter, 1981.

Richter, Dr. *Wilpilz Kochbuch.* Munich: Verlag Dr. Richter, 1981.

Richter, Nora. *Champignon Kochbuch.* Munich: Verlag Dr. Richter, 1981.

————. *Die Schonsten Gerichte,* Munich: Verlag Dr. Richter, 1981.

Rolf, R. T., and F. W. Rolf. *The Romance of the Fungus World.* New York: Dover, 1924.

Sass, John E. *Botanical Microtechnique.* Ames: Iowa State University Press, 3rd ed., 1958.

Shaffer, Robert L. *Keys to Genera of Higher Fungi.* Ann Arbor: University of Michigan Biological Station, 1968.

Singer, Rolf. *Agaricales in Modern Taxonomy.* Tucuman, Argentina: Universidad Nacional de Tucuman, 1949.

Smith, A. H., and L. R. Hesler. *The North American Species of Pholiota.* New York: Hafner Publishing Co., 1968.

Smith, Helen V., and A. H. Smith. *The Non-Gilled Fleshy Fungi.* Dubuque: William C. Brown, 1973.

Snell, W. H., and E. A. Dick. *The Boleti of Northeast North America.* Lehre: J. Cramer, 1970.

————. *A Glossary of Mycology.* Cambridge, Mass.: Harvard University Press, 1971.

Stevens, R. B. *Mycology Guidebook.* Seattle: University of Washington Press, 1974.

Tosco, Uberto. *La Cueillette des Champignons.* Paris: Grange Battelliere, 1969.

United States Department of Commerce. *The ISCC-N.B.S. Method of Designating Colors and a Dictionary of Color Names.* Washington, D.C.: National Bureau of Standards, 1955.

Von Frieden, Lucius. *Mushrooms of the World.* New York: Bobbs-Merrill, 1969.

Wasson, R. Gordon. *The Wondrous Mushroom.* New York: McGraw-Hill, 1980.

————. Soma: *The Divine Mushroom.* New York: Harcourt, Brace and World, 1968.

Wells, V. L., and P. E. Kempton. *A Preliminary Study of Clavariadelphus in North America.* Ann Arbor: Michigan Botanist, 1968.

Wilczek, Lech. *Grzbow Jest w Brod.* Warsaw: Nasza Ksiegarnia, 1967.

Zeitlmayer, Limus. *Knaurs Pilzbuch.* Berlin: Droemersche Verlag, 1955.

CURRENT AMERICAN FIELD GUIDES

Aurora, David. *All That the Rain Promises and More. . . .* Berkeley: Ten Speed Press, 1991.

————. *Mushrooms Demystified.* San Francisco: Ten Speed Press, 1986.

Bessette, Alan, and W. J. Sundberg. *Mushrooms: A Quick Reference Guide to Mushrooms of North America.* New York: Macmillan, 1987.

Bessette, Alan E. *Mushrooms of the Adirondacks.* Utica, N.Y.: Country Books, 1988.

Bessette, Arleen Rainis, and Alan Bessette. *Taming the Wild Mushroom: A Culinary Guide to Market Foraging.* Austin: The University of Texas Press, 1993.

Christensen, Clyde M. *Edible Mushrooms,* 2d ed. Minneapolis: University of Minnesota Press, 1981.

Coker, W. C., and A. H. Beers. *The Boleti of North Carolina.* Chapel Hill: University of North Carolina Press, 1943.

————. *The Stipitate Hydnums of the United States.* Chapel Hill: University of North Carolina Press, 1951.

Dickinson, Colin, and John Lucas. *The Encyclopedia of Mushrooms.* New York: G. P. Putnam's Sons, 1979.

Fisher, Alexander H., and Bessette, Alan. *Edible Wild Mushrooms of North America.* 1992.

Glick, Phyllis G. *The Mushroom Trail Guide.* New York: Holt, Rinehart & Winston, 1979.

Groves, J. Walton. *Edible and Poisonous Mushrooms of Canada.* Ottawa: Canada Department of Agriculture, 1962.

Hard, M. E. *Mushrooms, Edible and Otherwise.* New York: Hafner Publishing Co., 1961.

Harris, Bob. *Growing Shiitake Commer-*

cially. Madison: Science Tech Publishers, 1986.

——. *Growing Wild Mushrooms.* Berkeley: Wingbow Press, 1976.

Hesler, L. R. *Entoloma in Southeastern America.* Berlin: J. Cramer, 1967.

Horn, Richard Kay, and Dean Abel. *A Guide to Kansas Mushrooms.* Lawrence: University of Kansas Press, 1993.

Huffman, Donald M., L. H. Tiffany, and G. Knaphus. *Mushrooms and Other Fungi of the Midcontinental United States.* Ames: Iowa State University Press, 1989.

Hurley, Jean. *Mushrooms of the Northeastern Woods: A Visual Guide.* North Conway, N.H.: Birchfield Books, 1983.

Katsaros, Peter. *Familiar Mushrooms of North America: The Audubon Society Pocket Guide.* New York: Knopf, 1990.

Kibby, Geoffrey. *Mushrooms and Other Fungi: American Nature Guides.* New York: Smithmark Publishers, 1992.

Largent, David. L. *How to Identify Mushrooms to Genus II: Macroscopic Features.* Eureka, Calif.: Mad River Press, n.d.

Largent, David. L., and H. P. Thiers. *How to Identify Mushrooms to Genus II: Field Identification of Genera.* Eureka, Calif.: Mad River Press, n.d.

Largent, David L., David Johnson, and Roy Watling. *How to Identify Mushrooms to Genus III: Microscopic Features.* Eureka, Calif.: Mad River Press, n.d.

Lincoff, Gary. *The Audubon Society Field Guide to North American Mushrooms.* New York: Knopf, 1981.

——. *Simon & Schuster's Guide to Mushrooms.* New York: Simon & Schuster, 1988.

Marshall, Nina L. *The Mushroom Book.* New York: Doubleday, 1902.

McKenny, Margaret, D. E. Stuntz, and J. F. Ammirati. *The New Savory Wild Mushroom.* Seattle: University of Washington Press, 1987.

McKnight, Kent and Vera. *A Field Guide to Mushrooms.* Boston: Houghton Mifflin Co., 1987.

Metzler, S. and V. *Texas Mushrooms: A Field Guide.* 1992.

McIlvaine, Charles. *One Thousand American Fungi.* Indianapolis: Bowen-Merrill, 1990.

Miller, Orson K. *Mushrooms of North America.* New York: E. P. Dutton, 1978.

Orr, Robert T., and Dorothy B. *Mushrooms of Western North America.* Berkeley: University of California Press, 1979.

Oetker, Dr. A. *Pilz Kochbuch.* Bielefeld: Verlag Rudolf A. Oetker, 1963.

Pacioni, Giovanni. *Guide to Mushrooms.* New York: Simon & Schuster, 1981.

Pearson, Lorentz C. *The Mushroom Manual.* Happy Camp, Calif.: Naturegraph Publishers, 1987.

Phillips, Roger. *Mushrooms of North America.* Boston: Little, Brown, 1991.

Rinaldi, A., and V. Tyndalo. *The Complete Book of Mushrooms.* New York: Crown, 1972.

Seymour, Jacqueline. *Mushrooms and Toadstools.* New York: Crescent Books, 1978.

Smith, Alexander H. *A Field Guide to Western Mushrooms.* Ann Arbor: University of Michigan Press, 1975.

——. *The Mushroom Hunter's Field Guide.* Ann Arbor: University of Michigan Press, 1974.

——. *Mushrooms in Their Natural Habitat,* 2 vols. Portland, Oregon: Sawyer's, 1949.

——. *North American Species of Mycena.* Ann Arbor: University of Michigan Press, 1947.

——. *North American Species of Psathyrella.* New York: Memoirs of the New York Botanical Garden, 1972.

Smith, Alexander H., H. V. Smith, and Nancy S. Weber. *How to Know the Gilled Mushrooms.* Dubuque, Iowa: William C. Brown, 1979.

Smith, Alexander H., and H. Thiers. *The Boletes of Michigan.* Ann Arbor: University of Michigan Press, 1971.

Stamets, Paul. *The Mushroom Cultivator.* Olympia, Wash.: Asamkow Press, 1983.

States, Jack S. *Mushrooms and Truffles of the Southwest.* Tucson: University of Arizona Press, 1990.

Stubbs, Ansel H. *Wild Mushrooms Worth Knowing.* Kansas City, Mo.: The Lowell Press, n.d.

Stuntz, Daniel E. *How to Identify Mushrooms to Genus iv: Keys to Families and Genera.* Eureka, Calif.: Mad River Press, n.d.

Tekiela, Stan, and Karen Shanberg. *Start Mushrooming—The Easiest Way to Start Collecting 6 Edible Mushrooms.* Cambridge, Minn.: Adventure Publications, n.d.

Wasson, R. Gordon. Soma: *The Divine Mushroom.* New York: Harcourt, Brace and World, 1968.

Watling, Roy. *How to Identify Mushrooms to Genus IV: Cultural and Developmental Features.* Eureka, Calif.: Mad River Press, n.d.

Weber, Nancy S., and Alexander H. Smith. *A Field Guide to Southern Mushrooms.* Ann Arbor: University of Michigan Press, 1985.

Willard, Terry. *The Reishi Mushroom: Herb of Spiritual Potency and Medical Wonder.* Vancouver, B.C.: Sylvan Press, 1990.

INDEX

DESIGNED BY JIM WAGEMAN

TYPEFACES IN THIS BOOK ARE GARAMOND NO. 3, DESIGNED BY MORRIS F. BENTON AND T.M. CLELAND
AND BASED ON EARLIER MODELS BY CLAUDE GARAMOND AND JEAN JANNON,
DANTE, DESIGNED BY GIOVANNI MARDERSTEIG, AND
TRAJAN, DESIGNED BY CAROL TWOMBLEY
THE TYPE WAS SET BY BARBARA STURMAN, NEW YORK

PRINTED AND BOUND BY TOPPAN PRINTING
COMPANY, LTD., TOKYO, JAPAN